National Geographic Society
Washington, D.C.

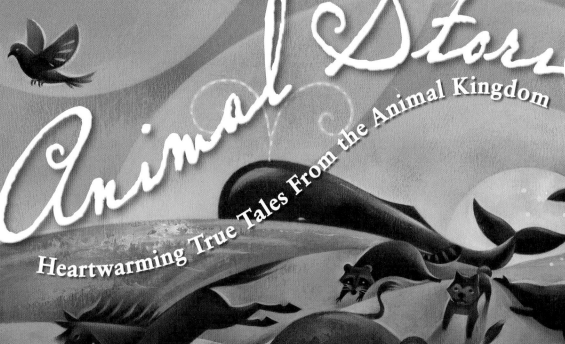

Animal Stories

Heartwarming True Tales From the Animal Kingdom

JANE YOLEN with her children,
HEIDI E.Y. STEMPLE, ADAM STEMPLE,
& JASON STEMPLE

ILLUSTRATED BY JUI ISHIDA

Table of Contents

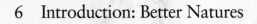

Better Natures

Even from the earliest days, humans and animals have had interesting, supportive, and sometimes difficult partnerships. They have hunted one another and worshipped one another.

For millennia, oxen have been harnessed for pulling, cows and goats have given milk, sheep have been sheared for their wool, cats bred to keep down vermin, dogs used for hunting and rescue, elephants for hauling, horses for riding. Animals have been our companions in home and farm, in work and war.

All our years on Earth we have loved animals, feared them, found them entertaining and dangerous, loyal and calculating, fawning and standoffish—and always mysterious. We walk the Earth with animals. Coexisting, but not full equals. Our natures and needs divide us, our language keeps us apart. Our human skills, opposable thumbs, bigger brains have made us lord over them when we should instead simply share this planet we all call home.

There are many times when the animals have surprised us with their humanity, or rather, with their better natures, helping out humans without expecting anything in return. And nothing brings us together more quickly and less selfishly than responding to an animal in peril or understanding how animals have saved our lives. Perhaps we should look to them more often than we do for meaning, for a helping hand, for love.

These stories represent a few—nineteen—of those times when animals surprised us, or we surprised ourselves by working with animals for the betterment of their situation and our own natures. We have chosen these stories specifically because they interested us, amused us, made us think and smile and sometimes cry. We hope you feel the same way.

Jane Yolen & the Stemple family

The Sled Dog Who Helped Save the Children of Nome

A litter of Siberian huskies was born in Alaska in 1919. One was a charming dark male with a white patch on his chest, a white "stocking" on his right leg.

His new owner named him Balto, after the Sami explorer Samuel Balto who had been part of the first recorded crossing of the interior of Greenland, and who helped introduce reindeer into Alaska. Balto was a name all Alaskans remembered and cherished. Soon they would come to know the name anew.

Trained to pull a sled, Balto soon showed his skills in a team—eager, hardworking, always willing to go that extra mile. But he didn't become a lead dog until six years later, in 1925. And because he led the final team into Nome on that particular trip, everyone knew his name.

In January of that year, the doctors of Nome, in the territory that would later become Alaska, realized that a deadly respiratory disease—diphtheria—was poised to devastate the town's children. Diphtheria was highly contagious and almost always fatal in those days. Today, most young children get a vaccine shot against it and so it has all but disappeared in the developed world. But back in 1925, no

Balto and his littermates were born in Alaska. No one could have predicted what a famous dog he would become.

Sled dog teams were the only way to get the lifesaving serum to Nome.

such shot existed. The only antitoxin serum was in Anchorage, nearly 700 miles (1,127 km) away from the last train station in Nenana.

Seven hundred miles—over rough terrain in the middle of an Alaska winter well before highways existed, before big semitrucks, before fleets of bush airplanes. In fact, there was only one possible plane in Anchorage, and when it

was hauled out of its winter storage for the trip, the pilot found that the engine was frozen solid.

An epidemic does not wait for people to build roads, to invent large trucks, to have planes flown up from Canada or the United States. The only way to get the serum to Nome in time—and it was a chancy way at best—was by dogsled.

The doctors in Anchorage and Nome conferred by telegraph. If the children of Nome were to have a chance, the trek had to begin at once.

A single dog team could not make such a trip without stopping for a night's rest, and that would eat up much needed time. There would have to be a relay of dogs, of sleds, of men.

The beginning of the trip with the serum was by train to Nenana, where the first of the more than 20 mushers who would make the trip lived. A musher is the man who owns the sled and dog team.

But just as an epidemic doesn't follow human time, Alaska weather doesn't always cooperate either. There was a blizzard covering most of the trail, the temperature hovered close to 50 degrees below zero F (-45.5°C). Sled dogs can run well in that temperature, and the mushers were used to it, too, bundled up in fur-lined parkas, and fur-lined mittens and boots. But no doubt about it—the blizzard complicated everything.

The first musher set out into the teeth of the snarling storm and he and his dogs ran the first 50 miles (80.5 km) into Tolovana. From there the next musher guided his dog team another 30 miles (48 km). The next team went 28 miles (45 km). And so it went as mushers, dogs, sleds, and medicine made their slow, difficult way toward Nome.

Where was Balto, the hero dog, in all of this? He was waiting with his team near the end of the line.

The winds kicked up another notch, the temperatures dipped further down. Now heavy snow obscured the way. It was not only a race against time but a race against nature.

One team startled a reindeer, and their lines became tangled. The musher, Henry Ivanoff, was still trying to untangle the dogs when he heard the sound of another team coming to greet them. Since the storm was growing fiercer, Ivanoff handed off the medicine packs to its musher, Leonhard Seppala.

Seppala sped off, trying to outrace the growing storm to get to the next checkpoint 91 miles (146 km) away. When at last his team came to Norton Sound, the water was clogged with ice. Going across the ice was the shortest way to Nome, but also the most dangerous. An ice pack can break up at any moment, especially with a heavy sled and dog team crossing it. The ice held long enough and Seppala passed the medicine to the next musher,

Charlie Olson, who in turn passed them to Gunnar Kaasen, whose lead dog was Balto.

Balto was not the only dog, he was part of a team. Some of the other dogs were Tillie, Fox, Sye, Billy, Old Moctoc, and Alaska Slim—13 dogs in all. They were supposed to have been the next-to-last team, but fortune—or misfortune—intervened.

Under Balto's leadership, the team made it to the next point with ease, but the final musher—who should have been ready to take over—was fast asleep, his dogs not ready for the trip. So Kaasen with Balto, and his teammates, raced on through the now-hurricane-force winds into Nome where they were greeted as heroes.

It had taken the 20 mushers and 150 dogs just over 127 hours of constant running to bring the serum to Nome, but they'd made it in time.

The children were saved.

Was Balto a hero? All the dogs in those teams

worked heroically, going through blizzards, across snow packs, through frigid conditions, racing as fast as their mushers asked, stopping infrequently and risking much. But because Balto's team—with Balto in the lead—arrived in Nome with the serum, he was proclaimed the hero of Nome.

Was that fair?

The dogs didn't care. They did what they

Balto and his team made it to Nome in time.

did for the joy of running, for the love of their teams, because they had trained hard under the musher's commands.

Balto was one of 150 heroes. He stood for all of them.

A year later, as a symbol for every dog who'd taken part in the epic run, a statue of Balto was erected in New York City's Central Park.

THE IDITAROD RACE COMMEMORATES THE RUN

In 1925, the only winter link between Anchorage and Nome was the Iditarod Trail. Only dog teams could be counted on to make the trip. Within ten years of the serum run, though, bush pilots would become the fastest, most consistent way of transporting people, food, and medical supplies during the long Alaska winters. But only the richest people could afford such travel. For the rest, dogsleds were still the only reliable transportation.

Thirty years later, the snowmobile changed the life of dogsled teams and mushers forever.

In 1964, the Iditarod Race was born as part of the 100th anniversary of Alaska's purchase from Russia. It also reminded people of sled dog culture and the Alaskan huskies, which had become a dying breed.

In 1985, Libby Riddles was the first woman to cross the finish line first, after 20 years of male winners.

Balanchine's Elephants

George Balanchine loved the ballet. He was first a dancer, then the most famous choreographer in the world. Early in the 1930s, he was brought to America to create an American school of ballet that would equal the famous schools of Europe. Balanchine worked with beautiful dancers—women so light on their feet they seemed to float through the air, and men so strong and graceful they almost defied gravity. He told stories through dance. If money was tight, his dancers wore simple costumes when they performed. When he became more famous, he could have any costume and any dancer he wanted for his companies. He collaborated with the most popular artists and musicians of the day for the stage and film.

Balanchine WAS ballet.

But in 1942, he was asked by John Ringling North of the Ringling Bros. and Barnum & Bailey Circus to create a ballet like no other ever danced. The stars of this new ballet wouldn't be Balanchine's dancers, they would be elephants.

Balanchine called his friend composer Igor Stravinsky. Would he

Balanchine worked with the most famous dancers of the day.

create music for this new ballet?

"For whom?" Stravinsky asked.

"For some elephants," Balanchine answered.

If this was an odd response, Stravinsky had an even odder reply.

"How old?"

"Very young," Balanchine answered.

"All right," said Stravinsky. "If they are very young elephants, I will do it."

And with that, Stravinsky, who—like Balanchine—was not afraid of a challenge or trying something new, got started on the music. He wrote a polka incorporating traditional circus instruments and a quick fun tempo. The music had some rhythmically jerky sections and offbeat harmonies.

People worried that it would upset the elephants, but that didn't stop Balanchine. Would the elephants be able to learn choreography? Would the dancers and the stars of the circus

be able to work together? If Balanchine was concerned about these things, he didn't show it.

Balanchine's wife, the lovely Vera Zorina, who was both a prima ballerina and movie star, would dance the lead in the ballet alongside Modoc, the largest Indian elephant in America.

Balanchine didn't exactly blend in at the circus. Like ballet itself, he was graceful and elegant. The circus was gritty and tough. But the gruff, cigar-smoking bullhands who tended

was a dancer for each elephant. Connie, who, truth be told, was afraid of the large creatures, was paired with an elephant named Ginny. The choreography called for her to balance on Ginny's trunk, look graceful, and, most important, not fall. But Connie kept falling. "You must try," Balanchine said to her gently, "to land on the balls of your feet, my dear."

Connie and the other dancers and the elephants learned Balanchine's choreography. They rehearsed while costumers cut 7,000 yards (6,400 m) of pastel fabric and sewed elephant-size tutus. Soon it was time to take the show on the road.

On April 9, 1942, the circus rolled into New York City, stopping first at Madison Square Garden. The audience filled the big top and read the program while they waited for the show. "Fifty Elephants and Fifty Beautiful Girls in an Original Choreographic Tour de Force. Featuring Modoc, premiere ballerina."

and trained the elephants seemed to soften when Balanchine was around. He was so soft-spoken and handsome that a young circus performer named Connie Clausen said—had he asked— she surely would have "walked into a cage full of hungry lions for him." The elephants, she thought, probably felt the same way.

Balanchine studied the elephants and how they moved, how they worked together, and how they learned. Then he began to set choreography. There

*Under the big top,
the dancers put on a
show to remember.*

They danced. First Modoc and Zorina together. Then girls and elephants in a corps de ballet like no one had ever seen before.

They toured 104 cities and performed 425 times. The *New York Times* said, "Modoc the Elephant danced with amazing grace, and in time to the tune, closing in perfect cadence with the crashing finale."

After the show closed, the circus and Balanchine parted ways. The ballet was adapted for dancers to perform without elephants. The music was adapted to be performed by a symphony. And the elephants toured with the circus doing circus things.

But elephants, they say, never forget. And, when it comes to ballet, it seems this is true. Even after they retired from the circus, the elephants were sometimes spotted—without music or tutus or trainers—dancing Balanchine's ballet.

THE HUMANE TREATMENT OF PERFORMING ANIMALS

Actor W. C. Fields famously said the first rule of show business is to never work with animals or children. But, really, animals (and children) have been part of show business for as long as people have been performing.

There are rules that govern the way performing animals must be treated, but, even so, many animals are abused in the name of entertainment. The American Humane Association, which can certify a movie as "No Animals Were Harmed" is a leader in performing animal protection. In addition, there are watchdog groups such as PAWS (Performing Animal Welfare Society) and PETA (People for the Ethical Treatment of Animals) that aim to make sure all animals are treated ethically and humanely, and they work hard to bring to justice those humans who cause animals harm.

Simon: Ship's Cat First Class

Everyone knows how much cats hate water. But not Simon, the cat on the British frigate H.M.S. *Amethyst*. He'd joined the ship's crew in peacetime, but it was during a war that he became famous, winning medals for bravery under fire.

Simon was born in 1947 on Stonecutters Island in Hong Kong, at that time a busy naval dockyard. He was black with white cheeks and chin, a white bib, and one white paw. When he was barely a year old, small and severely undernourished—certainly living wild—Simon was found by George Hickinbottom, a 17-year-old ordinary seaman, and a new member of the crew of the *Amethyst,* which had only recently docked at the island to resupply.

George liked cats and knew the ship needed one to help control the rat population. Rats can be a danger to a ship's food supply. They are also carriers of diseases, which can run rampant in the lower decks where the sailors sleep. George smuggled Simon on board, hiding the little cat in his tunic.

Simon quickly became a popular member of the crew. He turned out to be a fine ratter. He left "presents" of the dead rodents—or parts of

Simon joined the crew of the H.M.S. Amethyst.

them—on the sailors' beds as if saying, "Doing my duty!" He also took naps in the gold-braided hat of the ship's captain.

Captain Ian Griffiths was fond of the little cat, and he would even whistle him up to go on evening rounds, inspecting the ship together. But as kind as Griffiths was to Simon—or "Blackie," as he was sometimes called—the captain was tough on his crew. He warned George that if he saw any "cat muck" on the decks, he would have George "up on a charge."

When Captain Griffiths left the ship in 1948, he knew the sailors would miss Simon, so he left the little ship's cat (with George in charge) for the next captain, Lieutenant Commander Bernard Skinner.

Luckily the new captain was also a cat lover.

In April 1949, Skinner's orders were to take the ship up the Yangtze River from Shanghai to

Nanking to replace the duty ship there. It was to be a fateful trip.

Halfway upriver, the ship was fired on by Chinese guns. The first shots went wide, but an hour later another battery of guns opened fire, and this one caused the *Amethyst* to run aground. One

An explosion tore
through the ship.

before he could make it home. Twenty-five sailors were also killed in the attack.

Badly burned, Simon first hid in the cabin, but eventually he managed to crawl up on deck where some sailors spotted him and rushed him to the medical bay. His eyebrow whiskers had been singed off, and he was badly dehydrated. The ship's doctor removed four pieces of shrapnel from his leg and back and cleaned the burns, but no one expected Simon to last the night.

He did. After a miraculously short recovery, he went back to his duties—patrolling the lower deck for rats as well as visiting the sick and wounded sailors, which cheered them up enormously. The sailors viewed him as a hero, as they would have viewed a wounded doctor who still made his rounds.

But then a new captain, Lt. Cmdr. John Kerans, came aboard. He was not a cat lover and

of the very first rounds tore through the captain's cabin where Simon lay sleeping. The blast tore a 15-foot (4.5-m) hole in the wall.

Simon tried to run, but pieces of hot shrapnel hit him in the back and one leg, burning him as well. Captain Skinner was fatally wounded, dying

Simon was banished from his cabin. Eventually, though, Simon won over even the crusty Kerans.

When the ship got back to port, the sailors told the story of Simon and he became an instant celebrity, not only for being wounded in the battle, but also for how, as soon as he had healed enough, he had gone back to his two jobs aboard ship—keeping down the rat population and cheering up the crew. Stories were written about him not only in British newspapers but also in international journals and even in *Life* magazine.

Once the *Amethyst* reached Britain, it was announced that Simon was to be given the Dickin Medal, the animal equivalent of the British Medal of Valor. He was also to receive a Blue Cross Medal, the *Amethyst* Campaign Medal, and the made-up rank of "Able Seacat." Everywhere the *Amethyst* stopped on its way back to its home port in England, Simon was a star.

Simon became a decorated war hero.

All animals entering Britain in those days had to be put into quarantine, and kept away from local animals, to make sure they weren't bringing in any diseases. Alas, in the quarantine center Simon contracted a virus. The virus plus his war wounds were too much for the gallant little cat. He died on November 28, 1949, his medals awarded posthumously, which means given "after death."

His shipmates—and hundreds of well-wishers—turned up at Simon's funeral. His gravestone reads:

IN
MEMORY OF
"SIMON"
SERVED IN
H.M.S. AMETHYST
MAY 1948 — NOVEMBER 1949
AWARDED DICKIN MEDAL
AUGUST 1949
DIED 28TH NOVEMBER 1949.

THROUGHOUT THE YANGTZE INCIDENT
HIS BEHAVIOUR WAS OF
THE HIGHEST ORDER

OTHER ONBOARD CATS

Onboard cats go back to ancient times. Egyptians kept cats on their Nile boats. Trading ships of that time had cats, too, and introduced cats to Europe around 900 B.C. Some other famous ship's cats:

✷ Convoy, aboard the H.M.S. *Hermione*, even had his own tiny hammock for sleeping. He went down with his crewmates and ship when it was torpedoed in World War II by a German U-boat.

✷ Another cat, U-boat, lived on a Royal Navy vessel during World War II. Whenever his ship came into port, he'd take shore leave like the sailors, returning just before his ship sailed. One day, as the boat pulled away from the quay, U-boat came running down the dock, leaped over the water into the arms of the welcoming sailors, then sat down to casually wash himself.

✷ Trim was the cat who followed Captain Matthew Flinders from ship to ship as the captain mapped the coastline of Australia in 1802–1803.

Keiko, the Orca Movie Star

Around 1977 an orca was born in the chilly waters of the North Atlantic Ocean. His first couple of years were normal by orca standards, but in 1979 he was separated from his family and captured by fishermen off the coast of Iceland. The rest of his life would be anything but ordinary.

Then known as Kago, he was kept at Saedyrasfnid, an aquarium in Iceland, until 1982, when he was sold to Marineland, in Canada. At Marineland he was trained to perform for crowds of people. He was the youngest of the performing orcas and was bullied by some of his older tank mates. Because of this, he began to get skin lesions, infections that indicated this was an unhealthy environment for him.

A few years later, he was sold to Reino Aventura, an amusement park in Mexico City. Upon arrival, he was renamed Keiko, Japanese for "lucky one." Although Keiko quickly became a popular attraction, he could not have been feeling very lucky. At seven, Keiko was nearly 20 feet (6 m) long and the tank—which was designed for dolphins—was way too small. Besides, the tank water was too warm for an orca. While Keiko pleased crowds with five shows a day, as

A baby orca was born in the chilly waters of the North Atlantic Ocean.

time passed, he grew more and more unhealthy. Eventually, the park owners realized that its tank was too small and that Keiko would need a better home.

Finally, in 1992 it looked like the Lucky One's luck changed. Movie producers picked Keiko to be the star of their new film, *Free Willy*, a story about a young boy who helps an orca named Willy escape from a marine park and its horrible owner. *Free Willy* was a huge hit, but when fans of the movie learned of its star's health problems and living conditions, there was an uproar. Children all over the world wrote letters and made phone calls demanding that Keiko be set free.

Keiko's tank was too small for him. He would need a better home.

Real life, though, is not as simple as a Hollywood movie. Keiko had been taken from his family when he was only two years old and had never been taught the skills he would need to survive in the wild.

After much discussion, the park owners decided to build a new home for Keiko where he could get healthy and prepare for possible release into the ocean where he belonged.

With the help of animal rights groups and donations from Warner Bros. (the movie producers), an anonymous donor, and thousands of schoolchildren, the Free Willy–Keiko Foundation was formed. Reino Aventura donated Keiko to the foundation, which in turn joined together with the Oregon Coast Aquarium. Here, they would build Keiko a home the right size and begin his training for life in the ocean.

Keiko's larger tank was ready for him at the beginning of 1996. UPS donated a plane and delivered him in a huge crate full of cool water labeled with a large sticker reading "This Side Up."

Thousands lined the streets in Mexico to wish him well and millions watched his trip on television.

Keiko thrived in his new home, gaining almost 2,000 pounds (907 kg) in less than two years, and his lesions almost completely healed. As millions visited the aquarium to see him, Keiko was taught to catch and eat live fish.

Eventually, veterinarians and scientists decided he was ready to return to his home waters. They built Keiko a huge new pen and shipped it to a bay in Iceland close to where he last swam free.

On September 9, 1998, Keiko was loaded aboard a U.S. Air Force C-17 and flown back to Iceland. After 19 years, he was home and he appeared to love it.

Over the next year and a half, his trainers taught him to focus his attention underwater

Keiko began his long journey in free waters.

more and rely less on humans. As time passed, he continued to catch and eat more live fish.

In the spring of 2000, Keiko had his first taste of freedom, as he was encouraged to explore the bay outside his pen. Soon, he was taking regular ocean "walks," with his trainers following along in a boat. These led to longer stays in the open ocean and visits with wild pods of orcas. As two summers passed, Keiko continued to spend more time at sea alone and swimming with other orcas, but he never fully joined a pod, which worried the trainers, for orcas are very social animals.

Late in the summer of 2002, Keiko began the final leg of his epic journey. No one knows why, but over the next month and a half he swam nearly 1,000 miles (1,600 km), with no human contact, feeding himself on wild fish along the way. As he neared Norway, he followed a fishing boat into a fjord, seemingly eager for company. Soon, thousands of people flocked to the area

Free at last, Keiko enjoyed the attention of well-wishers.

to visit Keiko and celebrate his journey. He had so much attention that the government had to make new regulations so people would not swim near him or feed him. Until his death in 2003, Keiko remained in Norway, free to come and go as he pleased, but what pleased him seemed to be attention and company, so he spent a lot of time in the fjord in the company of humans.

Years later, people still argue about whether or not Keiko's journey back to the wild was a success. Some say that because he never joined a pod and eventually chose to return to the company of humans that the project was a failure. But, while it may not have been as perfect as a Hollywood movie ending, at the end of his story, Keiko was free.

ORCA (*ORCINUS ORCA*), KILLER WHALE?

Orcas, also known as killer whales, are not really whales at all; they are actually dolphins, the largest dolphins in the world. They can grow to 32 feet (9.75 m) and weigh an impressive 12,000 pounds (5,443 kg). Though they roam all of Earth's oceans, they prefer the colder waters near the Arctic and Antarctic. Living in family groups, known as pods, numbering from 5 to more than 30 orcas, they are very social creatures and constantly "talk" to one another, especially when hunting their prey. Each pod uses different sounds to communicate, distinct dialects similar to different human languages or accents.

Orcas dive regularly to 200 feet (61 m) deep for four to five minutes at a time while hunting. Their prey consists mostly of fish and marine mammals such as seals. They hunt together working as a team, earning them the nickname "wolves of the sea." Their distinct black-and-white patterns are unique to each individual. Scientists have photographed and identified thousands by their markings, keeping track of pods so they can tell if the populations are healthy.

Daughter of Sunshine

Binti Jua means "daughter of Sunshine" in Swahili, and in the summer of 1996, a gorilla named Binti Jua brought sunshine to the parents of a young boy in Illinois.

It was at the Brookfield Zoo in Brookfield, a suburb 14 miles (22.5 km) west of downtown Chicago. The zoo opened its doors in 1934 and immediately became a favorite visiting place for children and adults in the area. Brookfield was one of the first zoos in America to use moats and ditches instead of cages to separate the animals from humans and one another. It was the first in America to exhibit giant pandas and have an indoor dolphin facility. And it has always had a fine reputation for animal care, including successful brain surgery on a gorilla. In fact, the gorilla enclosure was an especially popular attraction.

One day in August, crowds gathered to watch the giant apes. In the press of people, a mother lost track of her three-year-old son. Before anyone could stop him, he had climbed the safety barrier that surrounded the enclosure. Then he fell over 20 feet (6 m), hitting the concrete floor hard and knocking himself out. There he lay, in with

Visitors at the Brookfield Zoo had no idea what drama was unfolding.

the gorillas, injured and unconscious as the great apes wandered over to investigate.

Gorillas are normally gentle and shy, but in unfamiliar situations their behavior can be unpredictable. Especially the males. And when they fight, they don't just hurt one another, they often hurt any females or babies near them as well. If any of the Brookfield gorillas got excited or angry near the injured boy, there was going to be a tragedy.

The crowd looked on helplessly as an eight-year-old female gorilla reached the boy. Her name was Binti Jua.

Binti Jua had been born in Ohio at the Columbus Zoo to parents Sunshine and Lulu and was moved to California as a youngster to be raised by zookeepers at the San Francisco Zoo. Gorillas raised by humans sometimes have trouble being mothers themselves, so when it came time for her to have babies, she was moved again, this time to Chicago's Brookfield Zoo to be taught how to act maternally.

Binti Jua held the unconscious boy, protecting him from the other gorillas.

The lessons must have worked, because when Binti Jua approached the injured boy, with her own 17-month-old baby, Koola, clinging to her, she seemed more curious than threatening.

Still, the crowd gasped in fear as she reached for the boy. But Binti Jua picked him up as gently as any mother would, cradling him in her arms. Some of the half dozen other gorillas in the enclosure tried to reach for him as well, but Binti Jua turned her back, protecting him with her own body.

Then she began moving toward the enclosure door that the zookeepers used. Three paramedics in the crowd rushed toward it. Other onlookers leaned far over the edge of the wall, considering jumping into the enclosure to help. But they didn't dare, fearful that they would spook the gorillas and the boy would be hurt.

At the door, Binti Jua laid the boy down and moved away, still keeping the other gorillas at bay. While onlookers snapped photographs and

took videos, the zookeepers and paramedics rushed in and carried the boy off to the hospital, where he recovered fully.

Binti Jua received an American Legion award and thousands of fan letters. One mother of three even sent the gorilla mom 25 pounds (11 kg) of bananas because she felt that "she deserved a reward."

Did Binti Jua know how heroic she had

The hero Binti Jua cuddled her own gorilla baby.

been? Evidently not. She took no notice of her newfound fame, content to while away her time in the gorilla enclosure eating gorilla chow (and the bananas) and raising Koola. She had a son a short while later, and now has a grandchild.

The parents of the boy kept their name out of the news. No one knows if he, today over 20 years old, ever returned to the zoo to say hello and thank-you to his protector.

And no one knows exactly why Binti Jua picked up the injured boy and protected him. Some say her training by humans kicked in when she saw him, and she carried him to where she carried her own babies to be treated by the keepers. Others say it is an example of how altruism in animals works. Perhaps she was just doing what any mother would do with an injured child: protecting him, comforting him, and getting him help.

ALTRUISM IN ANIMALS

Altruism—
the concern for the welfare of others.

Are animals capable of altruism? Dr. Frans de Waal thinks so. De Waal is a Dutch primatologist who works with apes and monkeys. He believes that empathy is not limited to humans alone.

"There's actually a lot of evidence in primates and other animals that they return favors," he says. They also share food, help each other, and protect their friends.

Some people think that apes are so much like humans that they need the same basic protections. The Great Ape Project (GAP) was formed in 1994 to "guarantee the basic rights to life, freedom and non-torture of the non-human great apes." Just as the Declaration of Independence declared American rights to the world, GAP members created the World Declaration on Great Primates for the rights of great apes. GAP believes apes are too intelligent and share too many human characteristics for them to be denied the same rights.

See *www.projetogap.org.br/en* and read the declaration for yourself.

Owen & Mzee: An Unlikely Pair

On December 26, 2004, trouble was brewing under the Indian Ocean. First the plates of the Earth slid, one under another. This caused a great shudder. An earthquake set the oceans rolling. A huge wave headed toward land. As it went, it got stronger and higher and gained speed. When it hit the coast from Africa to Thailand, the ocean was so strong it moved boats and cars and bridges and people. It flattened houses and trees and buildings. When the wave finally receded, it swept people and property back out with it, leaving devastation in its wake.

Just off the shore of the Kenyan village of Malindi, it left one orphaned hippopotamus all alone on a sandbar.

Suffering great losses themselves, the villagers could have ignored the stranded hippo. But they did not. Along with visitors who were on the beach that day, the villagers worked for hours trying to rescue the slippery, frightened animal. They finally restrained him in a net, but he wriggled free from the grips of his rescuers and tried to run away from them. One brave man, Owen Sobien, tackled him to the ground where the others were able to secure him with ropes and the net. The young hippo was saved.

A great wave hit the coast of Kenya, stranding a baby hippopotamus.

But where would he go? And who would be his family?

Dr. Paula Kahumbu of Haller Park—an old abandoned limestone quarry in Bamburi, Mombasa, Kenya, that had been made into a wildlife sanctuary—offered to take the baby hippo, now named Owen. Once he was at Haller Park, the staff would have to take care of him, since he couldn't be introduced to the other hippos, who would very likely attack him. Hippos may look friendly, but they can be territorial, fierce, and unfriendly. Even to other hippos. Even to baby hippos.

The long trip south to the sanctuary was not easy. Owen was distrustful of all the human attention he was getting. Finally, after being swept into the ocean, netted by the beach crowd, wrangled into a truck, and driven 50 miles (80.5 km) to Mombasa, Owen arrived at Haller Park. He was exhausted and afraid.

When the ropes that bound him came off, Owen was released into the *boma*—a fenced enclosure—that was to be his new home. He did what any scared baby hippo would do. He hid behind his mom. The problem was, the round gray creature he found to hide behind was not his mom.

Mzee, which means "wise old man" in Swahili, was a 130-year-old Aldabra giant tortoise, one of the largest tortoises in the world. He came from the Aldabra Islands in the Indian Ocean and was a cranky, slow-moving fellow with a cracked carapace, or shell—an injury he'd sustained when the last hippo he met tried to roll him around like a ball. Tortoises are not cuddly creatures. They are cold-blooded reptiles that don't nurture their young, let alone someone else's. Sometimes they live in herds, but, even then, they are solitary. So, when the 600-pound (272-kg) baby hippo tried to snuggle with him, Mzee wasn't really amused. In fact, he tried to get away. But where he went,

Much to the staff's surprise, Mzee seemed to tolerate Owen's company.

With visitors watching, the pair spent all their time together.

Owen followed. Owen, being bigger and faster, always caught up.

This went on all evening.

Finally, in the morning, it seemed Mzee had given up trying to escape Owen's attentions and a friendship began to form.

In the months that followed, the Haller Park staff was amazed and amused by the unlikely pair. They seemed to genuinely like each other. They ate their meals together. They swam together. Owen would observe Mzee and copy his behaviors. They even seemed to communicate, using grunting sounds, plus tugs, nips, and nuzzles.

People came to visit Haller Park. Lots of people. The whole world had fallen in love with Owen and Mzee. Their story was an inspiration. If such a strong friendship could be forged

No one could explain it fully, but Owen and Mzee became friends.

between these two animals that—at least on the surface—had nothing in common, perhaps there was hope for the human race.

Of course, Owen and Mzee didn't care about any of that. They were happy in their boma together and it didn't matter to them at all that Owen was a hippopotamus and Mzee was a tortoise. As far as they were concerned, they were a family.

OTHER UNLIKELY PAIRS

Interspecies friendships are not as uncommon as the expression "fighting like cats and dogs" would have you believe. In fact, there are so many stories about these unlikely couples that there are entire books and websites dedicated to them. You can find examples of friendships between a cat and owl, a rabbit and a deer, a dog and a dolphin, and an unlikely threesome made up of a lion, a tiger, and a bear, as well as many other odd pairings.

A number of the stories begin with an orphaned animal that needs a mother for food and protection. Sometimes, as in the case of Owen, the best mother isn't actually related—or female. Adoption isn't just for humans.

The Capitoline Geese

I n 390 B.C., the Roman Republic was a long way away from the giant empire it was to become. In fact, it might never have lasted past 390 B.C. if not for the actions of the most unlikely group of heroes in all history: a flock of geese.

The Roman Republic held Italy and part of Sicily. Large tribes of Gauls controlled almost every other land nearby. When a Roman ambassador sent to negotiate a treaty killed a chieftain of the Senones, the tribe quickly went to war.

The war did not go well for the Romans. At the Battle of the Allia, six Roman legions were defeated. The survivors retreated swiftly to Rome, so fast that they forgot to close the city gates behind them. Coming after them, the Senones swept in through the open gates and the Roman soldiers were forced to retreat even farther to the hill fort atop Capitoline Hill, one of the seven hills of Rome. It had high walls and cliffs, and try as they might, the Senones couldn't get in. The Senone army then surrounded the hill in a siege, while at the same time it tore the rest of the city down.

The Senones prepared to enter the city gates.

Life was hard on the besieged hill. The Romans had few supplies. Food was scarce. But even when the Romans got hungry, they didn't eat the sacred animals kept in the many local temples. And a good thing, too, because some of those animals were going to save their lives.

The siege went on for months. The Senones attacked a few times, but they were easily held back. They wanted badly to get atop this final hill and complete their destruction of Rome, but they couldn't find any way up.

During the siege, the hungry Romans did not resort to eating the sacred animals.

Actually, it was the Romans themselves who finally showed the Senones the way.

With most of the city destroyed, the surviving Romans were desperate to make contact with the rest of the republic to see if they could get help. But the same walls and cliffs that kept the Gauls out were keeping the Romans in. Finally, a Roman scout found a way. He climbed down the cliffs in the middle of the night and snuck out of the city without being seen by the Senones.

But the next day his tracks were seen.

The Senones quickly realized that what could be climbed down could just as easily be climbed up. So, on a dark night, they got their best troops together. They wrapped their weapons in thick cloth and covered any armor that might clank or jangle. The soldiers were ordered not to speak until they were past the walls and among the Romans. Then, silently, they began the climb.

They moved so silently, no Roman heard them: not the soldiers, not the sentries, not even the dogs bred to guard the walls. It took most of the night, but the Senones were careful and quiet and they were almost to the brow of the hill.

But at the very top, where the Senones were climbing, sat a temple dedicated to the Roman goddess Juno, patroness of Rome. And inside the temple, there was a flock of geese. Because the geese were sacred to Juno, the starving soldiers hadn't eaten them. In fact, some of the people had even helped to feed the geese, sharing their meager supplies so that the sacred geese could survive.

A good thing they had, because with the silent Senones almost into the Roman camp,

The Senone soldiers silently climbed the wall.

the Capitoline geese started to get uncomfortable.
When a goose gets uncomfortable, it starts
honking. And when one goose starts honking,
they all start honking. And when all the geese are
honking, they make such a racket, it could wake
a whole army.

Which is exactly what they did.

The noise first awoke Marcus Manlius, the
Captain of the Guard. Running to the cliff's edge,
he saw the Senones about to breach the walls.

*Alerted by the honking
geese, the Romans were
able to fight.*

He knocked the nearest one over the edge and attacked the rest. Awakened by the geese, the rest of the guard heard Marcus fighting and ran to help. One by one, the Senones were pushed off the cliff, their attack thwarted.

Marcus was rewarded for his bravery, first by the tribunes, and then by the soldiers. From their personal supplies, they each brought him a half pound of meal and a quarterpint of wine.

Hopefully, he shared some of it with the geese.

The Senone attack was thwarted by the Romans.

AFTER THE BATTLE

*A*fter the battle, both sides were ready to talk. The Romans offered to buy an end to the war with 1,000 pounds (450 kg) of gold. But when they were weighing the gold, they discovered that the Senones were using heavier weights to try to cheat them. The Romans complained, but Brennus, the Senone leader, wasn't impressed.

"Woe to the vanquished!" he shouted, and then he threw his sword onto the weighted side of the scale, making it even worse for the Romans.

Apparently, after defeating the Senones on Capitoline Hill, the Romans didn't feel vanquished. They attacked the Senones and, with help from a relief army, finally expelled the Gauls from Rome.

Hoover, the Talking Seal

On May 5, 1971, a local fisherman shot and killed a female seal near the Maine coast. Because seals were considered net robbers, fishermen dealt with them harshly. This practice was not uncommon in those days. The dead seal's four-month-old pup was found by another fisherman, George Henry Swallow III, and brought home to his wife, Alice Dunning Swallow. They decided to raise the little seal pup in their house in Cundys Harbor.

At first the Swallows kept the pup in their bathtub and tried to bottle-feed him. Whether he was in mourning for his mother, or frightened by his new surroundings, or just didn't like the bottle, he refused their offering. Still, within a day, the hungry pup was swallowing ground-up mackerel as if he were a vacuum cleaner. Laughingly, the Swallows named the pup Hoover after the popular vacuum cleaner brand.

Hoover soon outgrew the bathtub, so the Swallows moved him to a freshwater pond behind their house. When the neighborhood children found out, they visited daily to take Hoover for a ride in a wheelbarrow. One little girl kept telling him his name over and over in

Hoover refused a bottle but ate ground mackerel from a spoon.

her high little voice. This seemed to fascinate him.

Each day when George came back from fishing, he would get out of his car, hit the side with his hand, and yell toward the pond in his rough fisherman's voice, "Come over here." (Though to a non-Mainer, the phrase would have sounded like "Come ovah heah.")

Hoover would scamper to George's side, where George would greet him with "Hello there!"

Pretty soon the children were reporting to the Swallows that Hoover was talking to them, saying "Hello" and "Hello there" and "Come over here," all in a thick Maine accent.

Four months later, Hoover had grown so large and eaten so much fish, the Swallows couldn't afford to keep him any longer. But as Hoover had not lived in the wild since he was a pup, they were afraid to just let him go back into the ocean. After all, Hoover had absolutely no fear of humans. The Swallows were afraid he'd hang around the fishing

*Hoover greeted
George when he
returned from fishing.*

boats trying to talk to the fishermen and get shot.

So they took Hoover to the New England Aquarium in Boston, Massachusetts, where he became a great favorite. Besides the phrases he'd learned from the Cundys Harbor children and the Swallows, Hoover could say his name in a high-pitched child's voice as well as "How are ya" and "Get down," all accompanied by a gutteral laugh.

Did Hoover really talk? An aquarium visitor wrote this: "[A]round 1980, I went to the…aquarium and watched the seals in the pool outside. I thought that there was an old drunken man accosting people because I kept hearing "Hoovah, come ovah heah" over and over. It took me about five minutes to actually believe that it was the seal. It was bizarre because he would make eye contact as he was talking…The recordings do not do him justice, the technology was so rudimentary back then…He made everyone smile."

The animal trainers at the aquarium weren't sure Hoover actually knew what he was saying or what function those phrases served. Perhaps he was just mimicking sounds he'd heard as a pup. Perhaps he was looking for friendly applause and kind laughter. But whatever he meant, he sounded just like a person from Maine.

Hoover lived for 14 years at the aquarium, his story told by such publications as *Reader's Digest* and the *New Yorker.* He appeared on *Good Morning America* and other television programs. He was as famous as a seal could be, all because he could say some phrases and laugh with the humans who visited him.

Hoover died of an unknown cause on July 25, 1985, at his private pool at the aquarium. At the time of his death, he weighed 200 pounds (91 kg). Hoover fathered six pups. None of them inherited his ability to mimic human speech, though a grandson—Chagoda ("Chucky")—has been much more vocal. Still, Chucky has never learned any actual phrases.

The aquarium's memorial for Hoover reads: "Hoover has been our goodwill ambassador to the world. Regular visitors will surely miss his cheerful 'Hello there' when they visit."

TALKING ANIMALS

Human beings have complex voice boxes and it's rare for any animal to be able to really mimic what we say. We are capable of both speech and songs, we can make many kinds of animal sounds, and also imitate with ease the sounds of wind through the trees, a car horn honking, a siren, and thousands of other noises.

After us, birds are the best vocal changelings. They can sing, and some can also do an incredible range of mimicry. But their voice boxes (the syrinx) and their brains are very different from ours.

Another group of vocal learners are cetaceans—whales and dolphins. But they also have very different vocal equipment, not at all like humans. However, pinnipeds—seals, sea lions, and walruses—have brains and larynxes like ours. Walruses actually sing. As Natalie Angier wrote in the *New York Times:* "In full breeding tilt, the bulls sound like a circus, a construction site, a Road Runner cartoon. They whistle, beep, rasp, strum, bark and knock. They make bell tones, jackhammer drills, train-track clatters and the rubber-band *boing!* of Wile E. Coyote getting bonked on the head."

Greyfriars Bobby

onstable John Gray, called Auld Jock by all who knew him, needed a new watchdog. Every police officer, or bobby, had to have one. It was regulation.

Auld Jock spent nights patrolling the Old Town section of Edinburgh, Scotland, in the shadow of the castle that grew up out of the rocks above the city. Edinburgh, in the 1850s, with its pickpockets, thieves, and criminals of all kinds, could be a dangerous place.

The puppy Auld Jock found was a six-month-old Skye terrier. The breed is well suited for police work. The dogs are strong and protected against the cold, wet northern weather by a double coat. They are scrappy, smart, and very loyal. Auld Jock named his new watchdog Bobby, a fitting name for a police dog.

Auld Jock hadn't always been a constable. He started out life, like his father before him, as a gardener. But Scotland needed policemen more than gardeners. As an officer of the law, Auld Jock was well respected in Edinburgh. His little dog Bobby was always by his side.

For a time, the two patrolled the city together—Grassmarket, the Cattle Market, and the Greyfriars Kirkyard (churchyard). When the

In the shadow of Edinburgh Castle, Bobby and Auld Jock lived a simple life.

Bobby, the loyal friend, sat vigil at Auld Jock's grave.

guns atop Edinburgh Castle sounded the one o'clock hour, they would often stop for a meal beside the kirkyard at the restaurant of John Traill.

But in the long, cold winter of 1857, Auld Jock developed a cough. He became sicker and sicker until, in February, he died of tuberculosis. His faithful Bobby was, as always, by his side. A dog, it is said, is man's best friend. Auld Jock may have been gone, but his best friend Bobby did not abandon him.

After the funeral, Auld Jock was buried in the Greyfriars Kirkyard, where ordinary folk were buried among the rich and powerful. James Douglas, fourth Earl of Morton, was buried there, as was George "Bloody" Mackenzie, who, it was whispered, haunted the graveyard. Bars and locks at the gates and over the graves of the rich families helped discourage grave robbers who prowled at night. Dogs were not allowed. But Bobby was not deterred by rules, robbers, or ghosts.

When James Brown, the kirkyard caretaker, arrived to unlock the gates the morning after Auld Jock's burial, he was surprised to see Bobby sitting vigil by his master's fresh grave. James was not an unkind man, but it was his job to enforce the rules. So he shooed Bobby away.

The next morning, though, Bobby was back by his master's graveside. No amount of running the little dog out did any good. In the morning, James would arrive to find Bobby there by Auld Jock's grave.

Through rain and cold weather, Bobby remained a stalwart friend. When he heard the castle guns firing at one o'clock, he would leave the graveyard and find a meal at John Traill's restaurant, where he and Auld Jock had eaten together. Though John couldn't coax Bobby to abandon the kirkyard and live at the restaurant, he made sure the little dog never went hungry.

Bobby was looked after by the local residents, who gave him treats and built him a small shelter against the elements. James Brown kept an eye out for him. But, no matter who tried, Bobby refused to be taken in by anyone. Auld Jock was still his master and the kirkyard was now his home.

Still, dogs needed to be licensed. Having no living master to apply and pay the rather large fee for his license, Bobby was in danger of being rounded up with the other unlicensed dogs and taken to the pound. He was saved from this fate by the Lord Provost Sir William Chambers, who stepped in and paid the fee. On a special collar, he engraved the words "Greyfriars Bobby – from the Lord Provost, 1867, licensed."

Bobby lived this way until 1872. When he died, at age 16, he was buried in Greyfriars Kirkyard close to Auld Jock. A century and a half later, he is still beloved in Edinburgh. A statue was erected in his honor just outside the kirkyard gates. Tourists young and old visit the statue to take a picture or leave a token. Or they come to sit in the kirkyard as Bobby did for so many years.

On his own stone, which is usually surrounded by treats left by admirers—flowers, sticks, bones, and notes—Bobby is memorialized with these words: "Let his loyalty and devotion be a lesson to us all."

A statue stands near the gates of Greyfriars Kirkyard to honor Bobby.

MAN'S BEST FRIEND

There are several legends about Greyfriars Bobby—each contradicting the last. John Gray's age and profession as well as the cast of characters and facts change. But what remains constant in this story, which is a combination of the "histories," is that Bobby was a Skye terrier who, even after his master's death, was a loyal companion.

Bobby is not the only loyal dog in history. Outstanding among many others are Constantine, a German shepherd from Russia who made repeated pilgrimages to the spot he last saw his family after a car crash; Hachiko, a Japanese Akita who met his master's train for nine years after the professor's death; and, in Argentina, Capitan, a loyal German shepherd who still arrives at six every morning at the grave of his master who died in 2006.

The Elephant Whisperer

Long ago, the mighty Zulu warrior king Shaka had a private hunting ground called Thula Thula. It consisted of 5,000 acres (2,023 ha) of South African land.

Over the years, Thula Thula became a game preserve that was eventually bought by a famous conservationist known as the "elephant whisperer." His real name was Lawrence Anthony. He and his wife Francoise made Thula Thula their home. Also at home on the preserve were a wide variety of animals, including zebras, giraffes, white rhino, leopards, wildebeest, crocodiles.

One day in 1998, Anthony was called by an elephant welfare organization to adopt a herd of rogue elephants on another game preserve, some 600 miles (965.5 km) to the north. These elephants were "troublesome," the caller said.

How troublesome?

Over and over the elephants had broken through the preserve's electric fences, the matriarch—the female herd leader—twisting the wire with her tusks until the wire broke. Then the entire herd raced away, trampling fences, wandering onto farmland, destroying crops.

The wild elephants broke through the game preserve's electric fences.

Nobody else wanted those elephants. Anthony was their last hope. If he didn't take them, all the elephants—males, females, babies— would have to be shot.

Even though Thula Thula was not entirely operational, it never occurred to Anthony to say no. As he had only two weeks to build miles of boundary fences and a stockade strong enough to contain the herd, he got right to work.

Suddenly, word came that the elephants had once again broken out of their confinement and someone had shot both the matriarch and her baby. The other elephants were inconsolable, but had nevertheless been pushed into a gigantic trailer that was even then being driven to Thula Thula.

When they arrived, Anthony and his rangers gave the elephants medicine to calm them down, then opened the trailer doors. The huge new matriarch, Nana, emerged first, followed by her

Nobody *wanted the troublesome elephants. Anthony was their last hope.*

baby bull, and the rest of the herd. The men of
Thula Thula managed to corral them into the
giant enclosure where they would stay until ready
to be set loose into the large preserve.

But less than a day later, the elephants worked
together to fell a tree that smashed the fence, after
which they stomped on the electric generator till
it was—in Anthony's words—trampled "like a tin
can" and then they raced out of the stockade.

The herd went missing for two days. Local
wildlife authorities issued elephant guns to the
staff while local farmers began carrying large
caliber rifles. It was only a matter of time before
all the elephants would be wiped out unless they
could be made safe in Thula Thula.

Using a helicopter, Anthony and his rangers
found the herd, sedated the elephants, and drove
them back to the preserve.

Anthony knew that he had to win the
elephants' trust if they were to make Thula Thula

Anthony knew he had to win the elephants' trust.

their home, and the only way to do that was to live with them inside the enclosure, though there would be an electric fence between them for his safety. He was joined by his head ranger, David. They slept in the Land Rover, but otherwise stayed outside talking to the elephants, reassuring them. As Anthony wrote later, "We all had to get to know each other."

A month went by. Anthony hoped his plan was working. But waking one morning, he saw the mammoth shape of Nana and her baby staring at his car across the electric fence as if measuring its crushability.

On a hunch, he got out and walked slowly toward her. He trusted her, trusted the bond forming between them.

Nana reached carefully through the fence with her trunk. Anthony stood his ground. Nana's trunk explored his head, his hair, his clothes. In turn, he touched her trunk with his hand gently. It was the moment things changed for them. In some strange way they'd become friends.

In the years that followed, the elephants remained in the Thula Thula preserve, though they often ranged to the far reaches of the territory. But they always came back to Anthony's house, sometimes all but going into his living room.

When Nana gave birth to a son, she came right to the house to show off her new calf. When Anthony's first grandchild was born, he showed the baby to Nana.

The elephants roamed Thula Thula but always returned to Anthony's house.

But that is not the end of the story. Lawrence Anthony died young, at 61. The elephants of Thula Thula walked for 12 hours through the Zululand bush to reach the house. The herd arrived on the Sunday after he died. They stayed for two days mourning him.

How did they know he had died?

It's a great mystery. But Anthony's sons and wife witnessed their mourning and were grateful that their huge friends had come to say goodbye.

The herd stayed for two days mourning the elephant whisperer.

ELEPHANT MOURNERS

Elephants mourn their dead and there are even elephant graveyards where elephants mourn their kin. These beliefs, long part of elephant folklore, are only now being studied to see if such things are true.

Dr. Karen McComb, an expert in animal communication and cognition, and her colleagues have written their findings on elephants and mourning in the Royal Society journal *Biology Letters*. McComb writes: "Most mammals show only passing interest in the dead remains of their own or other species." In comparison, "African elephants are reported not only to exhibit unusual behaviors on encountering the bodies…becoming highly agitated and investigating them with the trunk and feet, but also to pay considerable attention to the skulls, ivory and associated bones of elephants that are long dead."

In one study, investigators showed 19 different family groups of elephants three objects: an elephant skull, a piece of ivory, a piece of wood. All the elephants showed a strong preference for the skull and the ivory, even rocking the ivory back and forth with their feet.

Cher Ami, the Pigeon Hero

When you think of an animal hero you might think of a fireman's dalmatian, or a policeman's German shepherd, or a warhorse. But animal heroes come in all shapes and sizes.

Cher Ami may have been just a little homing pigeon, but he is considered one of the great heroes of World War I.

Since the 1800s, the U.S. Army has included a division known as the Signal Corps. Its job is to help all of the United States' armed forces communicate. In the beginning, the Signal Corps used flags and torches to stay in touch, but over the years the corps helped to develop new ways to send messages, using radios, telegraphs, telephones. During World Wars I and II, they used carrier pigeons.

Homing pigeons are domestic pigeons that are specifically bred to be able to find their way home over distances of hundreds of miles. People have been flying homing pigeons for sport and communication for thousands of years. When the birds deliver messages, they are known as carrier pigeons. The sender takes the pigeon, usually in a cage, to wherever he or she is going. When it's time to send a

Cher Ami, a homing pigeon, was part of the U.S. Army Signal Corps.

message, a tiny piece of rolled paper is written upon, sometimes in code, and put in a small tube attached to the pigeon's leg. Then the sender releases the bird. The pigeon takes off and finds its way home to its loft, often hundreds of miles away, delivering the message.

During World War I, most of the pigeon lofts were kept with the commanders, and the senders (soldiers) would carry a few "war pigeons" with them into battle. The front lines of the war were always moving, so the lofts had to be mobile, initially built with wheels and later built directly onto trucks or buses so they could be where the action was. When needed, the soldiers would release a pigeon to deliver a message to their home loft.

Cher Ami delivered 12 such messages in his service, but it was his last message that made him famous.

In the fall of 1918, Cher Ami and many other war pigeons traveled with the U.S. Army's 77th

Division in a massive attack against the German Army in the Argonne Forest of France. Cher Ami's battalion was the only group to break through the German troops' strong front line. Now, the battalion of 554 men—with their few pigeons in mobile lofts—were cut off from the rest of their

As the Lost Battalion took fire, Cher Ami was sent with a message.

division and surrounded by the enemy.

The next few days, the "Lost Battalion," as it would later be known, fought fiercely, but it was massively outnumbered. Constantly under attack, the men had almost no food, and they had to crawl under gunfire to a stream for water. The worst of it came a few days in, when their own forces—unaware that they were there—bombed the area.

Many men had already been shot, hit by grenades, or taken captive, and now they were being hit with friendly fire. The commander of the battalion, Major Charles Whittlesey, had earlier

*Though wounded,
Cher Ami saved the
Lost Battalion.*

sent notes with two pigeons carrying pleas for support, but he feared they had been shot down. Among some of the fiercest fighting, Whittlesey called for their last pigeon, Cher Ami.

A note was neatly rolled and placed in a canister attached to his leg. It read: "We are along the road parallel 276.4. Our artillery is dropping a barrage directly on us. For heaven's sake stop it." Cher Ami took flight among exploding artillery and gunfire and was shot out of the sky almost immediately.

With life-threatening wounds, he took flight again, this time avoiding gunfire as he flew out of the Germans' range. He flew the 25 miles (40 km) back to his loft in 65 minutes, arriving covered in blood. Although he had been blinded in one eye and shot in the breast and leg, he delivered the lifesaving message.

The Americans immediately stopped bombing the Lost Battalion, but their battle waged on for

several days until reinforcements could break through the German line.

Cher Ami was credited with helping save the lives of the 194 soldiers who made it out alive.

Back at the base, army medics managed to save Cher Ami's life but not his leg. They carved him a leg out of wood and he returned to the United States by boat. He became the mascot for the Department of Service and was given the Croix de Guerre with Palm, a French military medal. He never fully recovered from his wounds and died an American hero in 1919. He was later inducted into the Racing Pigeon Hall of Fame, and a mounted specimen of Cher Ami, created by a taxidermist, is displayed at the Smithsonian National Museum of American History.

Following World War I, Cher Ami was celebrated in America as much as any other war hero.

HOMING PIGEONS: HOW DO THEY FIND THEIR WAY HOME?

Most birds have a strong homing instinct and many can migrate huge distances, returning to the same spot each year. The pigeon's homing instinct is extra strong, which has led humans to use them for many purposes throughout history. Ornithologists (scientists that research birds) have been studying how birds navigate for many years.

No one knows for sure exactly how the homing instinct works. It is likely that pigeons use a combination of sight, smell, and sound, as well as the ability to sense small changes in the Earth's magnetic field. Perhaps they use the magnetic field and visual clues—such as the sun and stars—as a kind of compass. When they are in a familiar area, pigeons may use their strong sense of smell and hearing to remember a "map" of their territory. They also may use visual landmarks, such as mountains and rivers. It is thought that individual birds may prefer to use some senses more than others and may therefore choose different paths home.

Washoe, the Hand-Signing Chimp

"*Y*ou, me out go.*" "OK, *but first clothes.*" (Washoe puts on a jacket.) "*What that?*" "*Shoe.*" "*Whose that shoe?*" "*Yours.*" "*What color?*" "*Black.*"

In 1965, a very young female chimpanzee was captured by a hunter in West Africa, then sold to the U.S. Air Force personnel for research in the space program. No one could have foreseen that 42 years later, Washoe, as she was named, would be world famous and rate an obituary in the *New York Times*—something kings and presidents and movie stars routinely expect but not animals. Yet that is exactly what happened.

In less than a year, Washoe was taken from the Air Force project by scientists Allen and Beatrix Gardner. Part of their plan was to teach her to speak with humans. There had been other such projects, but they'd always focused on teaching apes to talk. However these projects had always failed because apes have very different vocal apparatuses and make sounds in other ways. The Gardners had a different idea. Apes use a kind of hand-signing in addition to their vocalizations, so the Gardners, noticing the wonderful flexibility of a

Washoe was captured by a hunter and sold to the Air Force as a research chimpanzee.

chimp's body gestures, proposed teaching Washoe to use American Sign Language (ASL).

They also made what turned out to be the momentous decision not to treat Washoe as a lab animal, to be kept in a cage or locked up at night in a sterile laboratory, but rather to raise her like their own child, because chimpanzees in the wild live in close-knit families. As part of the experiment the Gardners pledged they would always sign to one another—not talk—when they were around her.

Washoe wore clothes and slept in a bed with sheets and blankets. She sat at the table with the Gardners when she ate. She had toys and books and an outdoor play center. She had dolls that she played with as a four- or five-year-old human child might—giving them baths, talking to them, acting out imaginary games. And she had regular chores as well. She lived with the Gardners until age five.

Washoe took to hand-signing at once. Her own name was formed with the three fingers raised in a W, flicking her ear with that hand.

Meanwhile, another couple—Deborah and Roger Fouts—had become part of the Washoe project in 1967 when Roger was a doctoral student and part-time researcher.

At first, most of the signs that Washoe learned were taught to her directly. But the Gardners and Fouts soon became aware that she learned other signs by observing them when they were signing among themselves.

All in all, Washoe learned about 350 ASL signs, but she and her later chimp friends also figured out how to combine the signs in ways to make new words. For example, when Washoe's friend Moja referred to a Thermos as "metal cup drink," that became its sign from then on. Washoe also taught her adopted son, Loulis, to sign without any help from the humans. The members of

the chimp family were observed on numerous occasions signing among themselves about feeling happy or sad, and could discuss objects not in the room at the time.

The Fouts had over the years become the ones who worked most directly with Washoe, so in 1971, after Roger had completed his doctorate, he and Deborah moved to the Institute for Primate Research in Norman, Oklahoma, and brought Washoe with them. The institute had other chimpanzees who became part of the project as well. Eventually, as academics will, they moved

Washoe and her family moved to a new home at Central Washington University.

again to Central Washington University in Ellensberg, Washington, in 1980 with their three children, because promises were made about a new research center.

Washoe and her chimp family came, too—Loulis, Moja, and later Moja's foster siblings, Dar and Tatu. Here the chimp family lived together, initially in a four-room, 3,600-square-foot (335-sq m) primate laboratory in the university's psychology building. Fouts made it clear that he chose Central over much more famous universities like Yale because at Central he would never be required to use the chimps for biomedical research.

Ten years later, the university had built a

wonderful new area for the chimps, and Washoe spent her last years in the new sanctuary. She romped with her family in the outdoor area, but also enjoyed looking through books, magazines, catalogs (especially shoe catalogs). Often she participated in coffee and tea parties with her human friends. Unlike her diet in the wild, Washoe got to enjoy such foods as oatmeal with onions, pumpkin pudding, and eggplant. She loved to chew gum.

When she fell ill in 2007, she was 42 years old. According to Roger Fouts, she was still signing up until the day of her death. At the memorial service, Fouts delivered the eulogy, saying, "I can still see the film of Washoe at about the age of three or four running quadrupedally (on four legs) to a crying Susan Nichols (Nichols had just had a difficult miscarriage), only switching to bipedal (two legs) running to sign "hug" to Susan as she approached."

The *New York Times* obituary celebrated her life, calling her, appropriately, "a chimp of many words."

ANOTHER FAMOUS SIGNING CHIMP

Nim Chimpsky, born eight years after Washoe, was taught signing in a study led by Professor Herbert Terrace. He wanted to prove Nim had a real language, not just a series of signs about objects he could see and touch and hold.

Nim mastered 125 signs, but Terrace concluded that Nim was only mimicking signs to win food or other rewards, not saying anything meaningful. It led to a long dispute with the Gardners and the Fouts, who said that the Nim project had been poorly conducted and that Nim had no emotional connection with the humans the way Washoe did. Also, they pointed out that the researchers were not adept at signing, and spoke verbally around Nim, thus isolating him from their conversation.

Professor Terrace abruptly ended the study and Nim was transferred back to the Institute for Primate Studies in Oklahoma, which then sold him to a pharmaceutical animal-testing lab. At last Nim was bought by the Black Beauty Ranch in Texas, operated by the Fund for Animals, where he retired.

Christian the Lion

The buyers for Harrods, London's largest department store, often found odd and fascinating things to put up for sale, but they really outdid themselves in 1969 by buying a lion cub from a defunct zoo park in Ilfracombe, England.

The cub, who they called Christian, turned out to be more than the store could handle. One night he escaped from his cage and destroyed several goatskin rugs in the carpet department.

So Harrods sold Christian to a pair of Australian friends, John Rendall and Anthony "Ace" Bourke, for 250 guineas, or about $500. At that time, Christian weighed 35 pounds (16 kg).

Rendall and Bourke, along with their girlfriends, cared for Christian in their London apartment, or flat, until he was a year old. They played with him, roughhoused and wrestled with him, let him sleep like a kitten in their beds.

But as lions will, Christian grew and grew until he was too big for the flat, and so the young men moved him to their furniture store, Sophistocat. They furnished the basement as his living quarters and took him for exercise runs in a local church graveyard. Occasionally,

Christian the Lion was sold by Harrods to John Rendall and Anthony Bourke.

they would go on outings to the beach.

Soon, though, Christian had reached 185 pounds (84 kg) and was still not full grown. Rendall and Bourke realized they weren't going to be able to keep him much longer, which made them very sad.

As luck would have it, the stars of the movie *Born Free,* Virginia McKenna and Bill Travers, came to the furniture store and met the lion. They gave the young men the address of African conservationists George and Joy Adamson, the people on whose lives *Born Free* had been based.

The Adamsons agreed to take Christian and introduce him into the wild.

Furthermore, McKenna and Travers let Christian stay in a huge, secure compound in their garden at their country home in Surrey until the Kenyan government allowed the young lion to be moved to Africa.

Once Christian was in Kenya, the Adamsons

Christian quickly grew too large to live with Ren-dall and Bourke.

picked him up and took him to the preserve they ran.

Integrating Christian into the wild wouldn't be easy. He'd never lived in Africa, never lived without human protection. He didn't have the hunting skills, didn't know the smells of the land. He had to be taught all of this.

George Adamson knew that Christian would have to first become part of a pride, a family group of lions. The male lions guard the pride and mark the territory, while the females do most of the hunting.

The first pride of lions the Adamsons tried to create for Christian included an older male lion named Boy and a female named Katania who was still a cub. But bad luck seemed to follow that first pride. Katania disappeared, possibly eaten by crocodiles at a watering hole. A second female was killed by rival lions. Boy was badly injured in the same attack and somehow lost his ability to interact with other lions or with

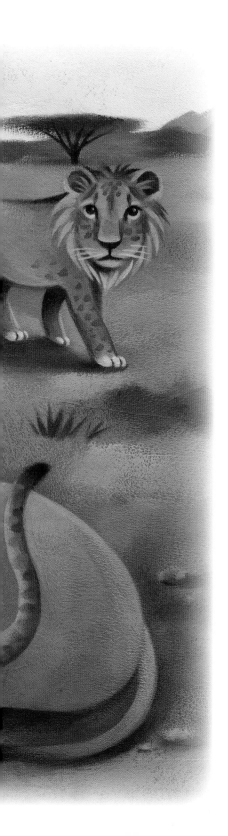

Christian settled in with a pride after a long adjustment period.

humans without fatal consequence. After he mauled an assistant, causing his death, George Adamson had no recourse but to put him down.

Adamson refused to give up on Christian, and eventually the new pride managed to settle down in a region around Kora National Reserve in Kenya.

Back in England, Rendall and Bourke could not forget their lion pal. A year later, having read of the success of the pride in newspaper articles, and knowing from correspondence with Adamson that Christian was now twice the size than when they last saw him, with cubs of his own, they wanted to visit him.

Adamson told them that coming to Africa would be useless as he hadn't spotted Christian and his pride for nine months. But Rendall and Bourke were adamant. They set the time of their arrival.

Surprisingly, the day before Rendall and Bourke's visit, much to Adamson's astonishment, Christian and his pride returned to the

compound. When the three men walked out into the bush, there was Christian and his family.

Rendall called out to the lion by name. Now fully grown, Christian stood and walked over to them slowly, as if uncertain. Then suddenly, convinced he knew them, the big lion began to run toward the men.

Rendall and Bourke didn't move, and Christian came up to them, standing on his hind legs to hug them just as he used to do as a growing cub, with his paws on their shoulders.

The reunion lasted until morning. Christian's

Christian greeted his former human friends with a lion-size hug.

lioness and cubs joined Rendall and Bourke, all of them sitting under the shade of a rock while Adamson videotaped the whole scene. The pride seemed to enjoy the attention of the two men who petted them.

As the sun rose, the pride left, melting away into the African landscape. It was the last time Rendall and Bourke ever saw Christian.

Christian and his pride returned to the wild after the reunion.

LIONS IN CAPTIVITY

Almost all captive lions live in zoos, some in extremely small cages. However, in the larger zoos most lions are housed in huge enclosures, with acres to run in. There are also a few lions in circuses, or those trained for movies. The reality, of course, is that as large as any enclosure, as nice as any trainer, the lions are not free.

However, in a zoo, a lion is protected, well fed, with access to health care. In captivity, a lion can live as long as 30 years; lions in the wild only live 10 to 15 years. In a world where lions are still being hunted, or killed by diseases such as distemper, some subspecies of lion are down to only about 300 members. Soon zoos may be the only places lions will be able to live in the world.

Saving the Whales

Hunting whales is how the native people (the Inupiat and Yupik) of the far northern land that is now Alaska have survived for many generations. Modern weapons of graphite and gunpowder now replace the traditional ivory harpoons, but the goal—harvesting whale blubber or muktuk—is still the same. The native people's relationship with the whale is steeped in history. The whale is not just a food source to the people. It is revered and respected even as it is hunted.

So on October 7, 1988, when whale hunter Roy Ahmaogak, who had just returned from a successful hunt, spotted three gray whales taking turns poking their heads out of one hole in the ice near Point Barrow, Alaska, his first thought was of respect for the trapped creatures.

Every spring, giant carcasses of whales that have become trapped under the autumn ice wash up and become part of the food chain, meals for a variety of other animals. Like the ones who perish each year, these three young, inexperienced whales had waited too long to start the 10,000-mile (16,000-km) round-trip to the warm waters of Baja California and back. They had remained just off the Alaska

Three whales were late in heading out to open water and became trapped under the ice.

coast, eating from the ocean floor in preparation for their migration fast. But winter had come early in 1988. And when the whales surfaced, they found themselves a long way from open water.

Roy could do nothing to help them. In fact, he couldn't even get close to their breathing hole, for the ice around it was thin and slushy. He went home and called the authorities—biologists who worked with the local population.

The next day, Roy returned with his whaling captain, a man called Malik. Malik's name fit him. It meant "little big man" and he was both—little in stature and big in reputation. Many believed Malik, the best whale hunter in generations, could speak with the whales. A true whale hunter kills only to sustain his village, never for money or glory. Malik and Roy knew these whales needed their help.

As it turned out, they weren't the only ones who wanted to save the whales.

Soon the biologists arrived. And the

Whale hunters Roy and Malik formed a bond with the whales and refused to give up on them.

reporters. News of the trapped whales—now named Putu, Siku, and Kanik—spread quickly. NOAA (the National Oceanic and Atmospheric Administration) sent a team, Greenpeace arrived, President Ronald Reagan assigned people to the crisis, and the Pentagon authorized the Alaska National Guard to respond. The oil companies offered help and sent equipment. Private citizens collected money and sent messages and suggestions. Companies sent chain saws and oil lamps and underwater pumps. One fourth-grade class in Arizona raised $75 to help.

Local residents, many of them native whale hunters, began cutting holes in the thick ice with chain saws. If they cut enough, perhaps the whales could swim along the path out to the open ocean. They knew that night was coming. Not the night that breaks when morning comes, but the Alaska night that begins when the sun sets in November and lasts until it rises again in late January.

The Russian icebreaker finally broke through the ice wall keeping the whales from open water.

The whales wouldn't survive the long night. The men cut more holes.

The biologists watched the whales cooperate—taking turns in the ice hole to breathe. All the people, too, cooperated—with tools and manpower. Reporters posted stories to the waiting world about everything that was happening there on the ice.

Around the globe, people mourned when the smallest whale, Kanik, stopped appearing in the hole to breathe. Now there were only two whales to save. Everyone worked even harder to free them.

As they cut the path of holes, the people knew they would have to cut through a wall of ice to truly free the whales. After every piece of equipment brought in failed to do the enormous job, a call was placed to the Soviet Union.

Two Russian icebreakers, large ships with the ability to ram through the Arctic ice, were about to head home from six months out at sea. It was the Cold War. The Soviets and the Americans were not friends. But—for the whales—they would come help.

The local men kept cutting holes. The press kept reporting on the progress and the Soviet icebreakers got ready to break ice. Once, twice, three times they rammed the wall of ice.

Finally the ice split. The whales had a path to freedom. Would they take it?

The whales made their way, swimming hole to hole toward the open water. Everyone was ordered off the ice and the press announced to the world that the whales were free! Reporters, photographers, and news crews packed up and went home.

But the whales hadn't left. In the morning,

GRAY WHALE

Whales are warm-blooded aquatic mammals. Even though they live in the water, they breathe air. Gray whales grow to 40 to 50 feet (12 to 15.25 m) long, can weigh up to 40 tons (36 MT), and can live to be 50 years old. They are usually covered with parasites and other organisms that make their heads look crusty. Every year they take on one of the longest migrations in the animal kingdom. Humans and orcas are the gray whale's only predators. The gray whale is a protected species, but it was removed from the endangered list in 1994. Whaling, or the killing of whales for their meat and blubber, is legal but highly regulated.

they were still there breathing through the quickly disappearing ice holes. Without the press watching, the people who remained—led by Malik—started opening up the holes again. When the sun set and they had to leave the ice, they hoped this time the whales would follow their path.

When morning came, the whales were gone. The crew of the Soviet icebreakers reported seeing them leave in the darkness.

It will never be known if they made it to the warm winter waters off Baja. But, whatever the rest of their journey held, they swam with the entire world cheering them on.

Seabiscuit, the People's Horse

He was a crooked-legged, undersized bay horse with a sad, drooping tail, the Cinderella of horses, who looked more like a loser than a winner. Prone to sleep too much, eat too much, he was so unimposing that no one considered that he had any chance in a race. As the *National Geographic* put it, he was "the poor man's horse from the other side of the tracks."

Of course, a lot of that underdog stuff was pure hype. Though his name was humble, Seabiscuit was not exactly of unknown stock. He was a descendant of the great racing horse Man O' War.

Born May 23, 1933, in Claiborne, Kentucky, Seabiscuit's first trainer—the legendary James "Sunny Jim" Fitzsimmons—thought Seabiscuit had potential but was too lazy to become a champion. Fitzsimmons proved correct, at least at the beginning. Seabiscuit lost his first 17 races and quickly became the joke of the stables.

As author Laura Hillenbrand put it, Seabiscuit's "gallop was so disorganized that he had a maddening tendency to whack himself in the front ankle with his own hind hoof."

But even being so ungainly, Seabiscuit began to win. Two races

The crooked-legged Seabiscuit lost his first 17 races.

at Naragansett Park, where he set a new course record, brought him some attention. By the time he was a three-year-old, he'd won almost $30,000 in prize money—a fortune in those days—before he was bought for the bargain price of $8,000. Most people thought his winnings were a fluke, in small races, against lesser horses.

The man who bought Seabiscuit was Charles Howard, a bicycle repair man turned multimillion-dollar car dealer. It was to be the best deal Howard ever made.

Of course, most of Howard's horsey friends thought it was no bargain at all. Only two people believed in the stumpy-legged horse: Howard's trainer, R. Thomas "Silent Tom" Smith, and a too tall, lower-level jockey named Johnny "Red" Pollard who was blind in one eye, a fact that he'd concealed for years so that he could keep riding.

An awkward-looking horse, a silent trainer, and a half-blind jockey. Hardly a trio that looked ready to win the biggest racing purses of the world.

Slowly, under Silent Tom's loving but strict tutoring, Seabiscuit began to improve. Tom even slept in Seabiscuit's stall to make the bond with the horse unbreakable. Seabiscuit had animal companions as well: a small cowpony named Pumpkin, a stray dog called Pocatell, and Jojo the spider monkey. A strange crew indeed.

As he got used to his new situation, Seabiscuit won race after race. Pollard—who could hardly see how far ahead or behind the other horses were—was Seabiscuit's jockey for almost all of them.

Seabiscuit began to win race after race.

Things seemed to be going along well, and then fate took a hand. Pollard fell from another horse he was riding, shattering his collarbone, breaking his shoulder, fracturing his ribs. He would not be allowed to ride again for a year.

A year in a winning racehorse's life is precious. So another jockey—George Woolf—got to ride Seabiscuit in what became known both as the "Match of the Century" and the "Race of Two Worlds": Seabiscuit versus War Admiral. This particular race had been set up because of the American Depression, when the rift between the rich and poor had grown enormous. The contest represented the rich versus the poor, the haves versus the have nots, the bankers versus the poor folk. Seabiscuit became the mascot for those on the have-not side, who wanted him to win to show the world that, in America, there was always a second chance.

War Admiral was already a Triple Crown champion known for his speed from the gate. Seabiscuit tended to hold back until near the end. The stands at Pimlico Race Course in Maryland were jammed with fans, an estimated 40,000 of them. Forty million more listened to the race on the radio.

Was Seabiscuit the favorite? He was the underdog, by a one-to-four margin. But what no one knew was that Silent Tom Smith had been secretly training Seabiscuit to run a new race from the start, with a burst of speed out of the gate. When the bell rang, knock-kneed Seabiscuit broke away from War Admiral. By the time War Admiral got over his surprise, he had to work hard to pull even, then got slightly ahead. Seeing his rival for the first time, Seabiscuit got a new charge and shot ahead once again, until he'd won by four clear lengths.

From his hospital bed, Pollard listened to the race on the radio, calling out, "Get going, Biscuit! Get 'em, you old devil!" After the win, he exclaimed, "He made a rear admiral out of War Admiral."

Seabiscuit was named American Horse of the Year for 1938 and was called the year's number one newsmaker as well.

Months later, Seabiscuit stumbled in a race and hurt his leg. No one believed he would ever race again. No one but Red Pollard. The two of them recovered together at Howard's ranch.

In 1940, half-blind Pollard returned to racing and rode Seabiscuit in the one big race that the

WHY WAS SEABISCUIT SO POPULAR?

By the time Seabiscuit was born, America had slipped into the Great Depression, a severe economic downturn that lasted until the middle of the 1940s. Cities around the world were hit hard, farm crop prices fell by 60 percent, unemployment rose to 25 percent. The poor got poorer and even the rich suffered.

So when a knock-kneed horse began to win against horses owned by bankers, the ordinary people had a four-legged hero to believe in.

The newspapers, magazines, and radio in 1938—this was before television— covered the Seabiscuit story more often than they covered President Roosevelt, Adolf Hitler, or Benito Mussolini, even as World War II began.

homely horse had never won—California's Santa Anita. Seventy-five thousand people were there to watch, while even more listened from home. Though Seabiscuit seemed uncertain at first, he made a final charge for the finish line and won with people screaming his name all the way home.

Smokey, the Firefighting Bear

n 1950, in the Capitan Mountains of New Mexico, a huge forest fire was burning. Soldiers from Texas were brought in to help fight the flames. In the midst of the devastation, they discovered a three-month-old cub clinging to a charred tree. He was all alone, and his paws were badly burned. The soldiers named him Hotfoot Teddy, and he was taken to Santa Fe to be nursed back to health.

Hotfoot Teddy's story spread quickly and he was recruited by the U.S. Forest Service to become their mascot.

Since 1944, the Forest Service had been represented by its cartoon mascot, American icon Smokey Bear. Hotfoot Teddy, the rescued cub, was about to become the "real" Smokey Bear. Flown all the way across the country, he arrived at his new home in Washington, D.C.

The Forest Service, founded in 1891, has always had preventing and fighting forest fires at the forefront of its mission. America's forests were long considered a national treasure and an important resource, so protecting them was of great concern.

However, it wasn't until World War II that the cartoon Smokey Bear was created. While forest fires had always been a problem,

Firefighting soldiers rescued a bear cub from a tree during a New Mexico forest fire.

World War II brought the threat directly into the public eye.

When Japan attacked Hawaii's Pearl Harbor, America joined the war and the government began to worry seriously about an attack on the U.S. mainland. The fear was that an attack on the West Coast could spark massive wildfires in the heavily forested mountains along the Pacific coastline.

Those fears weren't foolish. Japan had already mounted several attacks besides that on Pearl Harbor, including bombings by a submarine-launched floatplane in Oregon in which hundreds of balloons loaded with bombs had been sent up with the sole purpose to start forest fires. In addition, forest fires would have been especially problematic then, since most of the American firefighters were overseas fighting in the war. So with the security of the nation in mind, the Forest Service began an advertising campaign with posters to encourage people to be more careful in or near the woods, not to start campfires in or near the woods, and to be vigilant in case America's enemies started fires.

About that time, Walt Disney loaned Bambi's image to the Forest Service and a Bambi poster had been a great success following the very popular movie. But the loan had only been for a year. The Forest Service needed a new and permanent spokes-character. And so, on August 9, 1944, the cartoon character Smokey Bear was born. He was introduced to the public on his first poster later in October, depicted extinguishing a campfire with a bucket of water. The caption read, "Smokey says…Care <u>will</u> prevent 9 out of 10 forest fires!"

Smokey became the longest-running public service campaign in history, with almost everyone in the country recognizing him and understanding his message. He became so

Through a public service campaign, Smokey (the) Bear became a household name.

popular that he began popping up everywhere. He appeared in cartoons and children's books and in 1952 a song about him even created a debate about his real name. When the song was written, the writers added "the" to Smokey's name simply because it fit the rhythm of the song better. Even though his name was never officially changed, many continue to call him Smokey the Bear to this day.

The real-life Smokey Bear—Hotfoot Teddy— became a popular attraction at the capital city's National Zoo. For years, he was visited by millions of people.

As Smokey got older, a mate named Goldie was brought in with the hopes that Smokey might have a son to take over his duties when he retired from the Forest Service, but Goldie and Smokey never had any cubs.

In 1971, another orphaned cub was found in the same woods where Smokey had been rescued years earlier. He was named Little Smokey and was brought to the National Zoo to eventually take over for Smokey.

Four years later, in 1975, the zoo held a press-filled retirement ceremony for Smokey. Little Smokey was renamed Smokey Bear II and officially took over Smokey's duties as the Forest Service's firefighting mascot.

Smokey's legend lives on as one of the most enduring characters ever to be created. He has been known as the guardian of our forests for

The cartoon bear Smokey teaches Americans about the dangers of forest fires. Smokey's latest poster is shown here.

decades and has saved countless trees and likely quite a few bears. What began as a publicity campaign had become real to people across the nation long before little Hotfoot Teddy was found. In the end, life imitated art and both worked together to help save America from fires.

WAS SMOKEY TOO GOOD AT FIRE PREVENTION?

Not all fires are bad, and some forestry scientists argue that Smokey and his anti–forest fire campaign have been too successful. That may sound a little odd, but some forests need fire for their long-term health. Many pine trees rely on fires to clear out the undergrowth to make way for new seedlings. Jack pines, a subspecies, will not release seeds from their cones unless exposed to fire. Small fires that regularly burn off the "fuel"—such as dry underbrush, dead trees, and leaves—save areas from the huge, devastating fires that can destroy whole forests as well as human interests. When fire has not touched a forest for many years, the abundance of such fuel becomes a hazard.

This is why the Forest Service and its firefighters fight fire with fire. They try to keep areas free of too much fuel by conducting regular controlled burns. These carefully watched fires burn off the underbrush, allowing new growth, helping our forests to be healthy and safe.

Pale Male, Big-City Hawk

ale Male was the first of his kind to join the eight
million human residents of New York City in
raising his children in an apartment house. Like other
New Yorkers, his story is one of love and loss and the gritty
determination it takes to survive in the City That Never Sleeps.
Unlike other New Yorkers, Pale Male is a red-tailed hawk.

New York streets are known for a lot of things, but unless you
count pigeons and rats and various bugs, wildlife is not one of them.
Only in the many parks—green oases in the middle of a desert of
skyscrapers—has wildlife regularly been found.

In the early 1990s, Pale Male appeared in Central Park and
changed all that.

Historically, peregrine falcons had been the only raptors nesting
outside the parks, on the high-rise buildings that mimic the cliffs
they use in the wild. Until Pale Male, red-tailed hawks had never
nested in the concrete part of the city, only in the parks.

When he first arrived in Manhattan, Pale Male was a year old.
Named by local bird-watcher and author Marie Winn for his white

*Pale Male took
up residence in an
unlikely place.*

breast and lighter than usual head, Pale Male
settled in Central Park and attempted to build a
nest in a tree. But he was so harassed by crows,
the true bird kings of the park, he abandoned that
nest, roosting instead on a nearby Fifth Avenue
building. Much like the wealthy and famous
residents there, he enjoyed spectacular views of the
park. But, unlike his human neighbors, he used the
view to find food among the abundant squirrels
and pigeons across the street.

Early the next spring, Pale Male courted a
female red-tail in Central Park. By now, the local
bird-watchers were Pale Male watchers, but now
people who'd never been interested in birds and
their courtships before were involved, too—
alerted by news stories about the pair. Someone
named the female First Love and it stuck.

Twice the hawks attempted to nest in
the park, but for unknown reasons were
unsuccessful, returning gratefully to the Fifth

Pale Male and his mate attempted to start a family.

Avenue space. Then First Love was injured and brought to the Raptor Trust, a facility that takes care of injured hawks.

Pale Male must have thought she'd died, for he was seen later that year courting a new mate, who he found in the park. The birders named her Chocolate, and the pair was spotted often on Fifth Avenue window ledges, as if checking out apartments.

As winter turned into spring, the hawks took turns flying sticks across the bustling street, building a nest on the 12th-floor cornice of a ritzy apartment building.

With the whole city keeping an eye on them through newspaper stories and TV news, they laid eggs, watching over them intently for two months, but the eggs never hatched. The hawks abandoned the nest and resumed a nestless life in the park. The next year, they rebuilt their nest on a window ledge and laid eggs with the same unfortunate results.

The eyasses were watched by birders, tourists, and the building's residents.

Another year went by and the pair tried again. This time, in late April, to the delight of the crowds below, three eyasses—baby hawks—hatched. Instantly, Pale Male and Chocolate became the most famous new parents in New York City. They doted over their brood, and Pale Male brought more and more meals to the nest from the park—pigeons, squirrels, rats—his trips recounted by TV, radio, and newspapers.

By June, all three nestlings had fledged, flying across the busy avenue into the trees of Central Park.

Later that year, Chocolate was killed by a car while hunting outside of the city. Red-tailed hawks often hunt in the short grass near busy roadways and this can be a dangerous undertaking. The following spring, Pale Male was seen with another female. The crowds couldn't believe it—she was First Love! Rehabilitated at last, she'd been released from the Raptor Trust and had found her way back to the park for an unlikely reunion.

Over the next two years, Pale Male and First Love raised five eyasses in their nest on the building, but again tragedy struck. First Love died after eating a poisoned pigeon. Pigeons and rats are considered pests in the city and are sometimes controlled with poison. Unfortunately this poison can be transferred up the food chain to the hawks.

Pale Male remained resilient. Over the next four years, he raised 11 more eyasses with his new mate Blue, before she disappeared in 2001. From 2002 to 2004, he hatched 7 chicks with another new mate, Lola.

Over the years, bird-watchers and tourists lovingly watched the hawks daily from the park, using binoculars and high-powered telescopes, but some of the building's human residents had grown tired of the attention, tired of the bloody bones and feathers left from the hawks' meals littering their street. Without warning, in December 2004 the building's management sent workers out to remove the nest and the spikes that held it in place.

The removal led to angry protests. The public demanded that the spikes be replaced so that the famous hawks could rebuild. After several weeks of protests and a media firestorm, the building's management agreed to replace the spikes and install a new cradle for the nest.

Lola and Pale Male rebuilt quickly but—despite repeated attempts—didn't hatch any eggs for the next five years.

In 2010, Lola disappeared and again Pale Male quickly found a new mate, Lima, and after she disappeared, Zena, and next, Octavia.

Along with his many mates, Pale Male has built a dynasty on Manhattan's high-rise ledges. His many offspring have also found local mates. Following his example, they, too, build nests on the concrete edges till there are now more than 30 pairs of red-tailed hawks raising high-rise broods. It's a rooftop dynasty that wouldn't have been possible without the concerned citizens and bird-watchers of New York.

Pale Male's descendants fly over the city.

RED-TAILED HAWKS OUTSIDE THE CITY

Red-tailed hawks are the most common hawks in the United States. They adapt well to many environments but prefer open areas with high perches. They sit calmly atop these perches for hours, focused on the ground for the slightest movement of their prey. Outside of New York City, they eat a variety of things, including mice, rabbits, birds, and snakes. The hawks are named for their brick-red tails, but their coloring can vary greatly; some birds are almost all chocolate brown, while others may be very pale with an almost all-white belly.

The Last of Lonesome George

The Galápagos Islands are 500 nautical miles (927 km) west of South America and are part of Ecuador. Formed by underwater volcanoes in a spot where three different ocean currents meet, the islands have an ecosystem unlike anywhere else in the world. Many unique species of animals make their homes there. But perhaps the most unusual of all was a tortoise called Lonesome George, a Pinta Island tortoise, which is a subspecies of Galápagos tortoise.

In 1535, the first sailors landed on the islands. They saw that the tortoises were slow and unafraid of humans. The big reptiles could also live for a long time on very little. This made them especially attractive to the sailors, who often ran short of food on long voyages. They carried tortoises onto their ships and kept them as walking food stores that, when needed, could be turned into meat and soup.

After that discovery, the Galápagos became a regular stop for sailors of all types: merchants, pirates, whalers. And every time ships visited the islands, the sailors took more tortoises away. They also (accidentally) left goats on the island that ate the same food as the tortoises and—equally accidentally—left rats that ate the

The Galápagos Islands were a favorite stop for merchants, whalers, pirates—and now ecotourists.

tortoise eggs. All the native animals suffered, but the tortoises' numbers dwindled so much that every subspecies of Galápagos tortoise became endangered. The Pinta Island variety became so rare that eventually there was only one left.

Lonesome George.

For a long time, no one knew about Lonesome George. They thought the Pinta Island tortoise had already become extinct. But in 1971, Joseph Vagvolgyi, a Hungarian scientist, spotted Lonesome George while studying snails on Pinta Island. He didn't realize what he was seeing because he was a snail expert, after all. He took a picture and thought nothing more of it. But the next year, at a dinner he was hosting for turtle expert Peter Pritchard he showed his fellow scientist the tortoise picture.

"I practically lost my teeth," Pritchard recalled.

Park rangers set up an expedition, and in 1972 they captured Lonesome George and moved him to the Charles Darwin Research Station on Santa

Until George was found, the Pinta Island tortoise was thought to be extinct.

Lonesome George became the symbol of conservation, helping save the Galápagos Islands.

Cruz Island. Though George had lived for more than 50 years on Pinta, it was no longer safe for him to be in the wild. Feral goats had destroyed the vegetation he ate, and if he stayed there he eventually would have starved.

Lonesome George wasn't lonesome for long. The scientists at the research station hoped to breed him with other tortoises to save the Pinta Island species. Upon arriving at the station, he was immediately paired with two females of a different tortoise species. The pairing was successful, and the females laid eggs. But the eggs never hatched.

The scientists kept trying, and—despite his name—Lonesome George had a lot of mates over the next 40 years. But sadly, none of the eggs his partners laid ever resulted in offspring. The Ecuadorian government even offered $10,000 to anyone who could find a suitable mate for him. The reward was never collected.

Lonesome George also had a lot of visitors.

Lonesome George lived to be more than 100 years old.

People came from all over the world to see the last Pinta Island tortoise. He was a celebrity. His picture was printed on T-shirts and buttons and bumper stickers. He became a symbol of conservation and of the islands that Charles Darwin made famous. George didn't know it, but he was helping to save those islands.

The damage done to the islands during the 19th century was massive. Invasive species and overhunting had wiped out many native species. Without big changes and new laws, many more would be lost as well. With Lonesome George as a symbol, the movement to save the Galápagos gained popularity.

Not everyone wanted the islands saved. Tighter environmental restrictions caused some businesses to suffer. In 1995, sea-cucumber fishermen surrounded the research center to protest new laws protecting the ecosystem. They chanted, "Death to Lonesome George!"

But George survived, and the laws were passed. Slowly, the Galápagos began to recover.

Ecotourism became the center of the economy, and the local businesses now helped the research center's efforts rather than protesting them. In 2003, the last of the feral goats that had been so devastating to George's territory were removed and Pinta was declared goat-free.

George could have been returned home, but the scientists were still trying to breed him. And besides,

DARWIN, EVOLUTION, & TORTOISES

n 1831, Charles Darwin embarked on a four-year expedition on Captain Robert Fitzroy's ship, the H.M.S. *Beagle*. It was Darwin's observations of the animals and birds during their five-week stop in the Galápagos Islands that led to his theory of evolution, though he didn't finish it until nearly 25 years later. He saw many kinds of tortoises on that trip, though whether he saw the father of Lonesome George is debatable. Probably the closest the two ever came together was when George was brought to the Charles Darwin Research Station on Santa Cruz Island 150 years after Darwin had lived.

as Fausto Llerena, his caretaker for over 40 years, said, "He was like a member of the family to me."

In 2012, after living more than a century, Lonesome George died. A local business put a blackboard in front of its shop that read, "We have witnessed extinction. Hopefully we will learn from it."

Lonesome George was truly one of a kind.

The Tamworth Two

he town of Malmesbury in Wiltshire, England, was granted royal borough status by Alfred the Great in A.D. 880, making it the oldest borough in England. In its long history, it has seen wars and battles and the death of kings. But nothing ever caused a bigger commotion in the town than a couple of small ginger pigs.

It was early January 1998. Arnaldo Dijulio was driving his lorry to the V & G Newman slaughterhouse in Malmesbury. He had two five-month-old pigs in the back. They were brother and sister from a tough, old breed called Tamworth. Reddish in color, they weighed a little over 100 pounds (45 kg) apiece. They had no names.

Dijulio pulled into the slaughterhouse and lined up for the delivery platform. When it was Dijulio's turn, a man with a clipboard would record the delivery. Two gloved workers would help unload the pigs; they were the ones who would guide the animals inside to be slaughtered. Dijulio expected to get about £80 ($133) total.

The pigs had other plans.

When Dijulio opened up his truck to unload them, the pigs rushed out. Dijulio tried to grab them. The gloved workers tried to grab them.

Two Tamworth pigs escaped the slaughterhouse.

Even the man with the clipboard tried to grab them. But all pigs are smart, and these two were fast as well. They avoided the outstretched hands of Dijulio and the slaughterhouse workers and ran. They ran past the delivery area and into the yard, avoiding more workers and other farmers in line.

Cows mooed and sheep bleated as though in support of the fleeing pair. The pigs ran until they reached the fence surrounding the slaughterhouse.

The fence was tall and strong and wide and specifically designed to keep animals inside the slaughterhouse yard. But it wasn't designed well enough to keep small, smart pigs in, because, somehow, they found a hole in the fence and wriggled through. They were out of the yard. They were out of the slaughterhouse. But they weren't yet out of danger.

Sir William Waller, a general during the English Civil War, called Malmesbury the best naturally defended inland location he had seen. It sits on a

The pigs swam away from their would-be capturers.

hilltop, guarded on almost all sides by rivers and cliffs. The two pigs were no sooner free of the slaughterhouse then they were faced with the icy waters of the River Avon.

The slaughterhouse fence wasn't designed to keep people in, so the slaughterhouse workers were over the fence and through the gate and after the pigs quickly, chasing them down to the water's edge.

Luckily, pigs are excellent swimmers. And Tamworth pigs are known for their tolerance for cold. With clutching hands closing in on them, the two young pigs jumped into the frigid waters and swam to the far bank. There they disappeared into the dense thickets of Tetbury Hill.

But their story was far from over.

As trackers combed the woods and gardens of Tetbury Hill searching for signs of the pigs, the local newspaper, the *Western Daily Press,* filed a humorous story on the escapees. Newspapers hate to be scooped, even on as small a story as

イギリス発！ブタの脱走劇

one on two porcine fugitives. Before long, outside media swarmed the town. Within days, a news helicopter was hovering over Malmesbury while journalists from as far away as America and Japan joined the multitudes stamping through the English countryside searching for pig tracks.

A week passed with no capture. The pigs were dubbed "Butch and Sundance" for their ability to escape the lawmen's clutches, just like the pair of legendary Western outlaws.

The locals—even the policemen searching for the pigs—expressed their support of the escape. When the pigs were spotted entering a thicket on Mr. Carl Saddler's land, he told the press: "They are welcome to stay here as long as they want. It's the perfect place for pigs and I'd be happy for them to root out some of this undergrowth." The Wiltshire police spokesperson said, jokingly, "These are obviously cunning and devious animals and it appears to be a well-planned escape."

The fugitive pigs became celebrities as they eluded capture.

But after a week of evading capture and foraging in forests, thickets, and gardens, Butch—who turned out to be female—was captured in the garden of Harold and Mary Clarke. Sundance escaped, but the next day a pair of dogs chased him into the open, where he was downed by three tranquilizer darts.

The authorities prepared to return Butch and Sundance to their owner, who said they would still go to the slaughterhouse. He needed that £80, after all. Lucky for him—and even luckier for the renegade pigs—the *Daily Mail* newspaper bought them and the exclusive rights to their story for a price that was never revealed. It was probably much more than £80.

The Tamworth Two, as they were later called, lived out the rest of their lives peacefully at the Rare Breeds Center in Kent, never knowing how close they had been to becoming bacon, nor how much of a stir they had caused in the oldest borough in England.

WHAT IS A TAMWORTH PIG?

The Tamworth breed of pigs came into being in 1812 when Sir Robert Peel —twice prime minister of the United Kingdom—imported Irish pigs and bred them with the local pigs on his farm in Tamworth. They were recognized as a separate breed by the Royal Agricultural Society in 1885 and were soon imported into America and Canada, doing especially well in the colder climes. Tamworths are outdoor pigs, bred to feed off the land, with long snouts for foraging and long legs for walking long distances. Their ginger-red coats give them protection from cold and sunburn and they are often referred to as "ginger Tamworths" because of their color. They are reported to be intelligent and resourceful, as the Tamworth Two certainly proved.

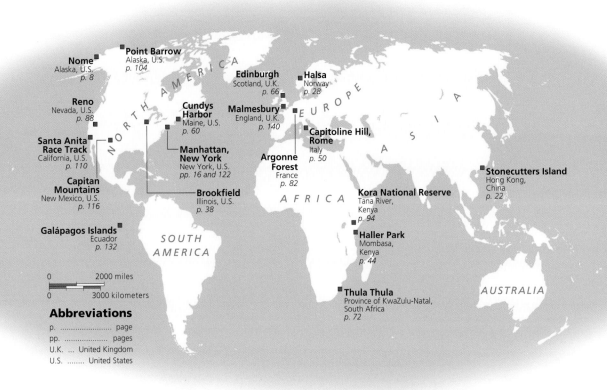

Point Barrow
Alaska, U.S.
p. 104

Nome
Alaska, U.S.
p. 8

Edinburgh
Scotland, U.K.
p. 66

Halsa
Norway
p. 28

Reno
Nevada, U.S.
p. 88

Cundys
Harbor
Maine, U.S.
p. 60

Malmesbury
England, U.K.
p. 140

NORTH AMERICA

EUROPE

ASIA

Santa Anita
Race Track
California, U.S.
p. 110

Manhattan,
New York
New York, U.S.
pp. 16 and 122

Capitoline Hill,
Rome
Italy
p. 50

Stonecutters Island
Hong Kong,
China
p. 22

Argonne
Forest
France
p. 82

Capitan
Mountains
New Mexico, U.S.
p. 116

Brookfield
Illinois, U.S.
p. 38

AFRICA

Kora National Reserve
Tana River,
Kenya
p. 94

Galápagos Islands
Ecuador
p. 132

SOUTH
AMERICA

Haller Park
Mombasa,
Kenya
p. 44

0   2000 miles

0   3000 kilometers

Thula Thula
Province of KwaZulu-Natal,
South Africa
p. 72

AUSTRALIA

Abbreviations

p. .... page
pp. .... pages
U.K. ... United Kingdom
U.S. .... United States

- **Nome, Alaska, U.S.:** Balto led a long, grueling run to deliver antitoxins to the children of Nome, saving their lives.
- **Madison Square Garden, Manhattan, New York, U.S.:** Balanchine's elephants performed their first ballet, the *Circus Polka*.
- **Stonecutters Island, Hong Kong, China:** Simon the ship's cat was born and later rescued by George Hickinbottom.

- **Halsa, Norway:** Keiko spent his life as a free whale in this Norwegian fjord, often performing tricks for the people who came to visit.
- **Brookfield Zoo, Brookfield, Illinois, U.S.:** Binti Jua saved a young boy who fell into the gorilla enclosure.
- **Haller Park, Bamburi, Mombasa, Kenya:** Owen and Mzee met and formed a very unlikely bond.

- **Capitoline Hill, Rome, Italy:** Geese saved an encampment of Roman soldiers from an attacking Gaul army.
- **Cundys Harbor, Maine, U.S.:** Hoover the seal lived with George and Alice Swallow, where he learned to mimic human speech.
- **Edinburgh, Scotland:** Greyfriars Bobby lived with Auld Jock, and later visited his grave in Greyfriars Kirkyard.

- **Thula Thula, Zululand, KwaZulu-Natal Province, South Africa:** Nana and her herd came to live at Lawrence Anthony's game reserve in South Africa.
- **Argonne Forest, France:** Cher Ami rescued a battalion of American soldiers stationed in the forest by successfully delivering a plea for help.

- **Reno, Nevada, U.S.:** Washoe lived with Allen and Beatrix Gardner and began to learn ASL.
- **Kora National Reserve, Tana River, Kenya:** Christian reunited with John Rendall and Anthony Bourke.
- **Point Barrow, Alaska, U.S.:** The U.S. and the U.S.S.R. combined forces to save two gray whales trapped under ice.
- **Santa Anita, California, U.S.:** Seabiscuit won his final race in the Santa Anita Handicap.
- **Capitan Mountains, New Mexico, U.S.:** Smokey Bear (Hotfoot Teddy) was discovered by firefighters.
- **Manhattan, New York, U.S.:** Pale Male was spotted in the city, much to the delight of New York bird-watchers.
- **Galápagos Islands:** Lonesome George was first discovered by Joseph Vagvolgyi.
- **Malmesbury, Wiltshire, England:** The Tamworth Two escaped their handler and the V & G Newman slaughterhouse.

390 B.C.
Geese defend the Romans stationed on Capitoline Hill from invading Gauls. The Roman Empire would go on to rule Western Europe until A.D. 476.

1857
Greyfriars Bobby visits the grave of Auld Jock for the first (but not the last) time. Their graves remain together in Greyfriars Kirkyard, which was first established in 1561 under the rule of Mary, Queen of Scots.

1918
Cher Ami delivers a message that saves the lives of the American soldiers stationed in the French Argonne Forest during World War I. World War I would continue until the signing of the Treaty of Versailles on June 28, 1919.

FEBRUARY 1, 1925
Balto leads the sled team that delivers diphtheria antitoxins to the children of Nome, Alaska. Balto was six years old when he made the run; he was born in 1919, right around the end of World War I.

1933
Seabiscuit is born in Claiborne, Kentucky. He became an unlikely symbol of hope to many Americans during the Great Depression, which lasted from 1929 to the early 1940s.

APRIL 9, 1942
Balanchine's elephants perform their first show at Madison Square Garden. The show helped the audience take their minds off of tough times, as the United States was currently involved in World War II.

1944
Smokey Bear becomes the mascot of the U.S. Forest Service. A real-life Smokey—Hotfoot Teddy—was found just in time for the Forest Service's 75th anniversary, which occurred seven years later in 1951. The Forest Service was originally created in 1876, under President Ulysses S. Grant.

1947
Simon, the ship's cat, is born on Stonecutters Island in Hong Kong. Simon later survived battle during the Yangtze Incident, which occurred when the H.M.S. *Amethyst* (Simon's ship) became stuck on the Yangtze River during the Chinese Civil War.

1965
Washoe is born in West Africa and taken to New York. She was originally captured by a hunter and sold to the U.S. Air Force to aid research for the space program—humankind first set foot on the moon just four years later, in 1969.

1971
Christian the lion is reunited with John Rendall and Anthony Bourke in Kenya. The space where Christian lived, Kora National Reserve, officially became a national park two years later in 1973, ten years after Kenya gained its independence.

TIME LINE
CONTINUED

MAY 5, 1971

George Henry Swallow III finds an orphaned seal pup, Hoover, and brings him home. Because of his unusual ability to copy human speech, Hoover became one of the first animal guests to appear on the American television show *Good Morning America,* which debuted in 1975.

1972

Lonesome George is rescued by a research team and taken to the Charles Darwin Research Station on Santa Cruz Island. Ten years prior, the Charles Darwin Research Station began the Galápagos conservation programs that are continued by the Galápagos National Park today.

OCTOBER 7, 1988

Roy Ahmaogak discovers three gray whales trapped underneath the ice off of Point Barrow, Alaska. Though the United States and the U.S.S.R. worked together to free the whales, the Cold War would continue for another year until the Malta Summit on December 3, 1989.

JULY 16, 1993

The movie starring Keiko, called *Free Willy,* is released in theaters. The technological boom of the 1990s enabled the following *Free Willy* movies to use animatronic whales, though Keiko was still credited for the role.

AUGUST 16, 1996

Binti Jua saves the life of a young boy who fell into the Brookfield Zoo's gorilla enclosure. At the time, Binti Jua had a daughter named Koola. She now also has a son and a granddaughter.

JANUARY 1998

The Tamworth Two escape captivity in Malmesbury, England. At the time of their escape, Malmesbury itself was over 1,000 years old, though people have lived in the area since 800 B.C.

DECEMBER 6, 2004

Owen is found on a sandbar in Malindi, Kenya. Owen was stranded by the tsunami resulting from the 2004 Indian Ocean earthquake, which registered an enormous magnitude of 9.1.

2004

Pale Male hatches seven chicks with his mate Lola. When the hawks' nest was removed from its building later that year, New Yorkers (including famous actress Mary Tyler Moore) led passionate protests to have the nest reinstated.

MAY 2012

Nana's herd journeys to Lawrence Anthony's house to honor him after his death. Anthony died shortly after the Thula Thula game reserve's 100th year; it is believed to be the oldest game reserve in KwaZulu-Natal.

BALTO, 8

In February 1925, Balto successfully led a team of sled dogs through raging blizzards and freezing temperatures to deliver much needed antitoxins to the children of Nome, Alaska. Balto was hailed as an American hero, touring much of the United States as a celebrity before happily spending the rest of his life in Cleveland, Ohio. To this day, Balto remains a symbol of perseverance and heroism; fans can pay tribute to his memory in New York's Central Park, where a bronze statue of Balto was erected in his honor. Visitors are also able to see a mounted specimen of Balto, prepared by a taxidermist, on display at the Cleveland Museum of Natural History in Cleveland, Ohio.

BALANCHINE'S ELEPHANTS, 16

In 1942 the Ringling Bros. and Barnum & Bailey Circus debuted a ballet like no other. Choreographed by George Balanchine and composed by Igor Stravinsky, the *Circus Polka* featured two types of dancers: professional ballerinas and elephants. Delighting audiences everywhere, the *Circus Polka* toured 104 cities and performed 425 times before the elephants retired. Although their days of performing were over, the retired elephants were known to spontaneously dance Balanchine's ballet from time to time. While there is no show quite like it today, audiences can still hear Stravinsky's original composition, watch performances of Balanchine's other works, and visit the ongoing Ringling Brothers circus shows.

SIMON, SHIP'S CAT, 22

Saved from his life as a stray by George Hickinbottom, Simon, a tuxedo-patterned cat, became an indispensible crew member of the H.M.S. *Amethyst* in 1947. Simon was known for his bravery and loyalty to the rest of the crew, and was awarded several medals after his valiant involvement during the Yangtze Incident. Unfortunately, Simon passed away after contracting a virus in quarantine. His shipmates—as well as many fans and admirers—all attended Simon's funeral, and Simon's grave can still be seen today at the PDSA Animal Cemetery in Ilford, Essex, England.

KEIKO, 28

Keiko spent the first few years of his life in a too small tank in Mexico City. After starring in the hit movie *Free Willy*, Keiko was rescued by the Free Willy–Keiko Foundation, with much help from fans, animal rights groups, and the *Free Willy* movie producers. Eventually, Keiko was freed off the coast of Iceland. He then made a solo journey to Norway, where he remained until his death in 2003. Today, a memorial for Keiko exists in Halsa, Norway, but Keiko's legacy reaches much further. The Free Willy–Keiko Foundation continues to raise awareness and support for the well-being of marine animals everywhere.

BINTI JUA, 38

It was the summer of 1996 when a young boy climbed the safety barrier at the Brookfield Zoo in Chicago, Illinois, and fell to the floor of the gorilla enclosure. Although the surrounding crowd feared the worst, what happened next was magical—eight-year-old gorilla Binti Jua gently picked up the boy and held him protectively until zookeepers were able to reach him and bring him to safety. Binti Jua was a hero, receiving the American Legion award and the thanks of parents everywhere. Today, she still lives happily at the Brookfield Zoo with her daughter, Koola.

OWEN & MZEE, 44

Following the great tsunami of 2004, villagers from the Kenyan village of Malindi rescued a stranded baby hippo. The hippo, now named Owen, was alone and confused and needed a friend. At Haller Park in Mombasa, Kenya, he found what he was looking for; unexpectedly, he became fast friends with an elderly turtle named Mzee. This unlikely friendship was a source of inspiration for people around the globe, proving that friendship and love can overcome great differences. Owen was eventually placed with a female hippo as he grew larger, but the bond that joined the two remains. Both Owen and Mzee still live at Haller Park.

THE CAPITOLINE GEESE, 50

During the early stages of the Roman Republic, Rome came under an assault from the fierce Gauls. Unable to match the Gauls in battle, a legion of Roman soldiers was forced to retreat to the Capitoline Hill, where they found themselves aided by unlikely allies—a flock of geese living in the Temple of Juno. When the attacking army attempted to climb the walls of the hill at night, the geese let out loud cries of alarm, alerting the Roman soldiers and allowing them to defend themselves. Travelers can still visit the Capitoline Hill in Rome, Italy, and view a frieze depicting the geese at the Museo Archeologico Ostiense.

HOOVER, 60

In 1971 orphaned seal pup Hoover came to live with Alice and George Swallow in Cundys Harbor, Maine. While having a pet seal is unusual enough on its own, Hoover soon began to imitate human sounds, greeting his owners and friends with "Come over here" and "Hello there!" Eventually, Hoover became too large to remain a pet, so he was transferred to the New England Aquarium in Boston, Massachusetts. Hoover became an instant celebrity, appearing on television and in newspapers, and his speech mimicry contributed greatly to research on pinniped vocalization. Although Hoover passed away in 1985, many of his descendants continue to live at the New England Aquarium.

GREYFRIARS BOBBY, 66

During the 1850s in Edinburgh, Scotland, Constable John "Auld Jock" Gray found himself a patrolling partner in the form of an abandoned Skye terrier puppy. Auld Jock and the terrier, Bobby, spent all of their time together, until Auld Jock passed away in 1857. But Bobby was still loyal—he remained by Auld Jock's grave day and night, leaving only to eat the meals that the local townsfolk offered him. After Bobby passed away, he was buried in the same graveyard next to his master. His love and loyalty continue to impress people to this day; both graves remain in the Greyfriars Kirkyard, and a statue stands in Bobby's honor just outside the gates.

THE ELEPHANT WHISPERER, 72

In 1998 conservationist Lawrence Anthony nearly met his match when he agreed to take on a herd of rogue elephants known for their troublemaking tendencies. At first it seemed as if nothing could calm the elephants and convince them to remain within the Thula Thula game preserve, but Lawrence's perseverance and kindness eventually won their trust. Sadly, Lawrence passed away at the age of 61. His death did not go unnoticed, however—led by their matriarch, Nana, the elephants formed a slow procession to Lawrence's house to mourn his passing. Thula Thula still houses many animals today, and Lawrence and his elephant tribe remain an inspiration for all.

CHER AMI, 82

Cher Ami was a carrier pigeon for the U.S. Army during World War I (like the one pictured at left). When the 77th Division found themselves stationed in the Argonne Forest of France and struck by friendly fire, they turned to Cher Ami to deliver a lifesaving message. Although he suffered life-threatening wounds from an artillery blast, Cher Ami successfully delivered the message, becoming a hero to many U.S. soldiers. Cher Ami's taxidermied, mounted specimen can still be seen at the Smithsonian National Museum of American History in Washington, D.C. The original telegram is also on display in Washington, D.C.; it can be seen at the National Archives.

WASHOE, 88

Over the years, many scientists have attempted to teach chimpanzees to communicate with humans by speaking or signing. However, no case has been quite as successful as that of Washoe the chimp, who came to learn more than 350 ASL signs. Raised by Allen and Beatrix Gardner, Washoe was able to communicate with both humans and other chimps through sign language. Washoe lived to be 42, and her passing was honored in the *New York Times* Obituaries section. Washoe's legacy also extends to modern research, such as the founding of the Great Ape Project in 1996.

CHRISTIAN THE LION, 94

In 1969 John Rendall and Anthony Bourke adopted the lion cub known as Christian from a department store. The pair grew to love Christian, but eventually sent him to the Kora National Reserve in Kenya so that he could live as a free lion.

One year later, Bourke and Rendall journeyed to Kenya to visit Christian and were greeted with a humongous hug from the lion, who remembered them even after his time in the wild. A video of the event went viral, mesmerizing viewers across the globe and inspiring animal conservationists. The Kora National Reserve went on to become a national park in 1989, and still exists as a refuge for wild animals.

PUTU, SIKU, AND KANIK, 104

In October 1988 a band of unlikely allies came together to save three gray whales trapped under ice off the Alaska coast. Thanks to private donations, media attention, the Alaska National Guard, and two Russian icebreakers, two of the three whales successfully made their way into the open waters. While the Cold War between the U.S.S.R. and America would continue into the next year, the world was heartened to see that two warring parties could come together for the sake of others. This also marked a turning point in the way that the public viewed whales, and whale conservation continues today.

SEABISCUIT, 110

As an unlikely underdog, Seabiscuit's rise to fame as a winning racehorse surprised and delighted America. Seabiscuit even recovered from an injury in 1939 to win the Santa Anita race in California. Seabiscuit retired a celebrity, and he continued to receive visitors at his home at Ridgewood Ranch for the rest of his life. To this day, many consider Seabiscuit a hero for underdogs everywhere, and fans can visit the statue dedicated to Seabiscuit in Santa Anita.

SMOKEY BEAR, 116

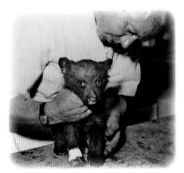

In 1950 firefighters in the Capitan Mountains of New Mexico discovered a bear cub with badly burned paws. Hotfoot Teddy, as he came to be known, was taken to Santa Fe to recover, and he was soon recruited by the U.S. Forest Service to become a firefighting mascot. Hotfoot Teddy was quickly hailed as the living incarnation of the wildly successful cartoon mascot, Smokey Bear, who was created in 1944. The real-life Smokey went on to live happily at the National Zoo in Washington, D.C. Although Hotfoot Teddy died in 1976, Smokey Bear lives on to this day, and continues his firefighting campaign.

PALE MALE, 122

Pale Male is a famous red-tailed hawk that has inhabited New York City since the early 1990s. Pale Male has inspired both bird-watchers and conservationists by his ability to overcome adversity and make a life in the city, including meeting mates and hatching chicks. Pale Male usually roosts on a Fifth Avenue building. His mates, chicks, and even other red-tailed hawks can still be spotted around the city.

LONESOME GEORGE, 132

The Pinta Island tortoise was long thought by scientists to be extinct. But in 1971 a Hungarian scientist discovered the last remaining tortoise of that species—Lonesome George. Lonesome George was brought to the Charles Darwin Research Station on Santa Cruz Island, another island in the Galápagos, where attempts to breed further Pinta Island tortoises were carried out. Sadly, none of the efforts were successful, and Lonesome George passed away in 2012.

However, Lonesome George inspired many to fight against the extinction of other species, and efforts by the nonprofits Galapagos Conservancy and Lonesome George & Co. continue today.

THE TAMWORTH TWO, 140

In 1998 two Tamworth pigs caused a stir by escaping the slaughterhouse and disappearing into the English borough of Malmesbury. The pigs were dubbed Butch and Sundance for their uncanny ability to evade authorities. They were finally caught, however, and lived out the rest of their lives peacefully at the Rare Breeds Centre in Kent. Their story has inspired lots of laughter, as well as a feature film. The staff at the Rare Breeds Centre are currently hoping to put up a plaque in memory of Butch and Sundance.

AUTHOR'S NOTE: THE FAMILY BUSINESS

We are a family of writers. Jane, our mom, published her first book 50 years ago—only a couple years before I was born. Adam, Jason, and I grew up with our writer mom and a scientist dad who was the person responsible for our love of the natural world. We were raised with one foot in literature and one in nature.

Even though I'm the oldest, I was the last to join the family business. Adam, a talented writer from early on, jumped in first, arranging piano scores for children's music books and later on writing novels and short stories. Jason, our artist, began illustrating books with his gorgeous photography. Both were pretty well established in children's books before I came on board. Though we have all worked with our mom on individual projects, this is our first book all together.

National Geographic first approached Jane (mom) with the idea for this book. But, since she was in the middle of a few large projects, she said she could only do it if we all worked together—something she had always wanted to do. We each chose stories and got to work researching. We made our decisions for both personal and practical reasons—I am a ballet mom and wanted to delve into the world of Balanchine; Adam loved the humor in the escapee pigs; Jason, a bird-watcher, found the story of Pale Male fascinating; and Jane, who chose the first piece—the elephant mourners—made sure we kept the subjects balanced.

We all have very different writing voices, which you will probably pick up on as you read the stories. Jane is the most lyrical, Adam, the funniest, Jason is our outdoorsman and more animal-centric in his writing. I am an out-loud writer—all staccato sentences and punctuation for reading aloud.

So, we each researched and wrote our own stories and then sent them to a central location (in our case, to Phoenix Farm, where Mom and I both work). There, she went over all the stories individually and I went over the book as a whole. Then came the rewriting. Each with our own stories and then with those of the others, we reordered and revised, polished and perfected the pieces until they all stood out individually yet still fit together as a whole. What you see in this book is the truest form of a collaboration: combining our interests, styles, and talents. As a family, we join in wishing you *Happy Reading.*

—HEIDI E.Y. STEMPLE
*on behalf of the
Yolen-Stemple family*

RESOURCES AND FURTHER READING

THE SLED DOG WHO HELPED SAVE THE CHILDREN OF NOME
"Balto." Central Park Conservancy. Available online at www.centralparknyc.org/visit/things-to-see/south-end/balto.html.

Balto and the Legacy of the Serum Run. Cleveland Museum of Natural History, 2013. Exhibition brochure. Available online at www.cmnh.org/CMNH/media/CMNH_Media/Balto/Balto__CMNH_update2013_02.pdf.

"Sled Dogs: An Alaskan Epic." *Nature,* season 18, episode 4, 1999. DVD. Available online at www.pbs.org/wnet/nature/episodes/sled-dogs-an-alaskan-epic/balto/3145/.

Miller, Debbie S. *The Great Serum Race: Blazing the Iditarod Trail.* Walker & Company, 2007.

Salisbury, Gay, and Laney Salisbury. *The Cruelest Miles: The Heroic Story of Dogs and Men in a Race against an Epidemic.* W. W. Norton & Company, 2003.

BALANCHINE'S ELEPHANTS
"George Balanchine: Master of the Dance." *American Masters,* 2004. DVD. Available online at www.pbs.org/wnet/americanmasters/episodes/george-balanchine/master-of-the-dance/529/.

Gottlieb, Robert. *George Balanchine: The Ballet Maker.* HarperCollins Publishers, 2004.

Kisselgoff, Anna. "Vera Zorina, 86, Is Dead; Ballerina for Balanchine." *New York Times,* April 12, 2003. Available online at www.nytimes.com/2003/04/12/arts/vera-zorina-86-is-dead-ballerina-for-balanchine.html.

Roy, Sanjoy. "Step-by-Step Guide to Dance: George Balanchine." *The Guardian,* July 30, 2009. Available online at www.guardian.co.uk/stage/2009/jul/30/dance-george-balanchine.

Schubert, Leda. *Ballet of the Elephants.* Roaring Brook Press, 2006.

Sheftman, Erica. "Vail Dance Festival: A Look 'UpClose' at Two Artistic Giants." *Vail Daily,* July 30, 2012. Available online at www.vaildaily.com/article/20120730/AE/120739996.

Taper, Bernard. *Balanchine: A Biography.* University of California Press, 1984.

SIMON: SHIP'S CAT FIRST CLASS
BBC News. "Wartime Hero Cat Simon Remembered." BBC News, 2007. Available online at http://news.bbc.co.uk/2/hi/uk_news/england/devon/7072669.stm.

Breyer, Melissa. "Cats at Sea: 7 Famous Seafaring Felines." Mother Nature Network, 2012. Available online at www.mnn.com/family/pets/stories/cats-at-sea-7-famous-seafaring-felines.

KEIKO: THE ORCA MOVIE STAR
"Keiko's Story: The Timeline." Free Willy-Keiko Foundation, 2003. Available online at keiko.com/history.html.

Garrett, Howard. "Keiko's Life." Orca Network, 2003. Available online at www.orcanetwork.org/captivity/keikostory.html.

Trivedi, Bijal P. "Killer Whale 'Willy' Shows Reluctance to Be Free." National Geographic News, September 10, 2001. Available online at news.nationalgeographic.com/news/2001/09/0910_TVwilly.html.

Winerip, Michael. "Retro Report: The Whale Who Would Not Be Freed." *New York Times,* September 16, 2013. Available online at www.nytimes.com/2013/09/16/booming/the-whale-who-would-not-be-freed.html?src=recg&_r=0.

DAUGHTER OF SUNSHINE
"From the Archives: Gorilla Protects Boy." NBC Chicago video, 2011. Available online at www.bing.com/videos/watch/video/from-the-archives-gorilla-protects-boy/1d2gkybtt.

King, Barbara J. "What Binti Jua Knew." *Washington Post,* August 14, 2008. Available online at www.washingtonpost.com/wp-dyn/content/article/2008/08/14/AR2008081403049.html?referrer=emailarticle.

Nickerson, Nancy. "Animal Hero: Binti Jua." The My Hero Project, 2013. Available online at www.myhero.com/go/hero.asp?hero=binti.

Schlesinger, Regine. "15 Years Ago Today: Gorilla Rescues Boy Who Fell in Ape Pit." CBS 2, Chicago, August 16, 2011. Available online at chicago.cbslocal.com/2011/08/16/15-years-ago-today-gorilla-rescues-boy-who-fell-in-ape-pit.

OWEN AND MZEE: AN UNLIKELY PAIR
"The Deadliest Tsunami in History?" National Geographic News, 2005. Available online at news.nationalgeographic.com/news/2004/12/1227_041226_tsunami.html.

Owen & Mzee (website). Turtle Pond Publications, 2008. Available online at www.owenandmzee.com/.

"Haller Park." Lafarge, 2013. Available online at www.lafarge.co.ke/wps/portal/ke/4_A_3-Haller_Park.

Chambers, Paul. *A Sheltered Life: The Unexpected History of the Giant Tortoise.* John Murray (Publishers), 2004.

Hatkoff, Isabella, Craig Hatkoff, and Dr. Paula Kahumbu. *Owen and Mzee: The True Story of a Remarkable Friendship.* Scholastic, 2006.

Hatkoff, Isabella, Craig Hatkoff, and Dr. Paula Kahumbu. *Owen and Mzee: The Language of Friendship.* Scholastic, 2007.

THE CAPITOLINE GEESE
"The Story of the Capitoline Geese." AncientWorlds LLC, 2002. Available online at www.ancientworlds.net/aw/Thread/1211592.

Livius, Titus. *History of Rome.* Book V. Trans. by Aubrey De Selincourt. Penguin Classics, 2002.

Weir, William. *50 Battles That Changed the World: The Conflicts That Most Influenced the Course of History.* New Page Books, 2004.

HOOVER, THE TALKING SEAL
"Hoover, the Talking Seal." New England Aquarium, 2013. Available online at www.neaq.org/animals_and_exhibits/exhibits/individual_exhibits/harbor_seals_exhibit/hoover.php.

"Hoover the Talking Seal." Audio clip. Posted on YouTube by the New England Aquarium, 2008. Available online at www.youtube.com/watch?v=prrMaLrkc5U.

Ralls, K., P. Fiorelli, and S. Gish. "Vocalizations and Vocal Mimicry in Captive Harbor Seals, Phoca vitulina." *Canadian Journal of Zoology,* 1985.

GREYFRIARS BOBBY
"Get to Know the Skye Terrier." American Kennel Club, 2007. Available online at www.akc.org/breeds/skye_terrier/index.cfm.

"The Story." Greyfriars Bobby, 2009. Available online at greyfriarsbobby.co.uk/story.html.

Atkinson, Eleanor. *Greyfriars Bobby.* Akasha Classics, 2008.

Kirkpatrick, Betty. *Greyfriars Bobby.* Crombie Jardine Publishing Limited, 2005.

Macgregor, Forbes. *Greyfriars Bobby: The Real Story at Last.* Gordon Wright Publishing, 1990.

THE ELEPHANT WHISPERER
The Elephant Whisperer (website). South African Game Reserve, 2011. Available online at www.theelephantwhisperer.com.

Lorenzi, Rossella (Discovery News). "Elephants Mourn Their Dead." ABC Science, November 4, 2005. Available online at www.abc.net.au/science/articles/2005/11/04/1497634.htm.

Martin, Douglas. "Lawrence Anthony, Baghdad Zoo Savior, Dies at 61." *New York Times,* March 12, 2012. Available online at www.nytimes.com/2012/03/12/world/africa/lawrence-anthony-baghdad-zoo-savior-dies-at-61.html.

CHER AMI, THE PIGEON HERO
"For Heavens Sake Stop It." Letters of Note, 2013. Available online at www.lettersofnote.com/2010/05/for-heavens-sake-stop-it.html.

Armed Forces History Collections. "Cher Ami—World War I Carrier Pigeon." *Smithsonian,* 2013. Available online at www.si.edu/Encyclopedia_SI/nmah/cherami.htm.

Webley, Kayla. "Top 10 Heroic Animals: Cher Ami the Pigeon." *Time,* 2011. Available online at content.time.com/time/specials/packages/completelist/0,29569,2059858,00.html.

WASHOE, THE HAND-SIGNING CHIMP
"Washoe." Friends of Washoe, 2013. Available online at www.friendsofwashoe.org/meet/washoe.html.

Carey, Benedict. "Washoe, a Chimp of Many Words, Dies at 42." *New York Times,* November 1, 2007. Available online at www.nytimes.com/2007/11/01/science/01chimp.html?_r=1&.

Gardner, R. Allen, Beatrix T. Garner, and Thomas E. Van Cantfort. *Teaching Sign Language to Chimpanzees.* State University of New York Press, 1989.

Perry, Nick. "'Signing' Chimp Washoe Broke Language Barrier." *Seattle Times,* November 1, 2007. Available online at seattletimes.com/html/localnews/2003986892_washoe01m.html.

Terrace, Herbert S. "Nim." *In Sign Language Studies,* vol. 30. Gallaudet University Press, 1981.

CHRISTIAN THE LION
A Lion Called Christian (website). Ace Bourke, 2013. Available online at www.alioncalledchristian.com.au.

Bourke, Anthony, John Rendall, and George Adamson. *A Lion Called Christian.* Broadway Books, 2010.

Moore, Victoria. "Christian, the Lion Who Lived in My London Living Room." *Daily Mail Online,* 2007. Available online at www.dailymail.co.uk/femail/article-452820/Christian-lion-lived-London-living-room.html.

Richardson, Justin, and Peter Parnell. *Christian, the Hugging Lion.* Simon & Schuster Books for Young Readers, 2010.

SAVING THE WHALES
"Gray Whale (Eshchritchtius Robustus)." National Geographic, 2013. Available online at animals.nationalgeographic.com/animals/mammals/gray-whale/.

Dorfman, Andrea. "Environment: Free at Last! Bon Voyage!" *Time,* November 7, 1988. Available online at content.time.com/time/magazine/article/0,9171,968853,00.html.

Mauer, Richard. "Unlikely Allies Rush to Free 3 Whales." *New York Times,* October 18, 1988. Available online at www.nytimes.com/1988/10/18/us/unlikely-allies-rush-to-free-3-whales.html.

Mauer, Richard. "Whales Break Out, Leave Trail in Slush." *Anchorage Daily News,* October 29, 1988. Available online at www.adn.com/1988/10/29/1470321whales-break-out-leave-trail-in.html#storylink=misearch.

Plowden, Campbell. "Operation Breakthrough: The True Story Behind Big Miracle." Greenpeace, 2013. Available online at www.greenpeace.org/usa/en/campaigns/oceans/whale-defenders/Operation-Breakthrough-The-story-behind-Big-Miracle.

Rose, Tom. *Freeing the Whales: How the Media Created the World's Greatest Non-Event.* Birch Lane Press, 1989.

Withrow, Dave. "NOAA'S Big Miracle Worker: NOAA Marine Mammal Biologist Dave Withrow and the Event That Inspired Hollywood." NOAA, 2012. Available online at www.nmfs.noaa.gov/stories/2012/02/2_1_2012_bigmiracle.html.

SEABISCUIT, THE PEOPLE'S HORSE
"Seabiscuit at Tanforan: Howard Horse to Start Training for Racing Comeback." *New York Times,* October 23, 1939. Available online at select.nytimes.com/gst/abstract.html?res=FA0E14F73F5A177A93C6AB178BD95F4D8385F9.

Hillenbrand, Laura. *Seabiscuit: An American Legend.* Random House, 2001.

Lovgren, Stefan. "From Nag to Riches: The Story of Seabiscuit." National Geographic News, 2003. Available online at news.nationalgeographic.com/news/2003/07/0728_030728_seabiscuit.html.

SMOKEY, THE FIREFIGHTING BEAR
"The Story of Smokey." Smokey Bear (website), Ad Council, 2013. Available online at www.smokeybear.com/vault/story_main.asp.

"Welcome to Smokey Bear Historical Park." New Mexico State Forestry, New Mexico Energy, Minerals and Natural Resources Department, 2013. Available online at www.smokeybearpark.com.

Anton, Mike. "At 65, Smokey Bear Is Still Fighting Fires." *Los Angeles Times,* July 24, 2009. Available online at www.latimes.com/news/science/environment/la-me-smokeybear24-2009jul24,0,7259761.story#axzz2mL4ZrZqo.

Baker, Robert D., Robert S. Maxwell, Victor H. Treat, and Henry C. Dethloff. *Timeless Heritage: A History of the Forest Service in the Southwest.* United States Dept. of Agriculture, 1988.

PALE MALE: BIG-CITY HAWK
"Red-Tailed Hawk." All About Birds (website), Cornell Lab of Ornithology, 2013. Available online at www.allaboutbirds.org/guide/Red-tailed_Hawk/id.

Lewis, James F. "History of the 5th Avenue Red-Tailed Hawk." The Legend of Pale Male (website), 2009. Available online at www.thelegendofpalemale.com/History.html.

Palemaleirregulars (blog), 2013. Available online at www.palemaleirregulars.blogspot.com.

Winn, Marie. *Red-Tails in Love: Pale Male's Story—A True Wildlife Drama in Central Park.* Vintage, 1999.

THE LAST OF LONESOME GEORGE
"Lonesome George." Galapagos Conservancy, 2012. Available online at www.galapagos.org/about_galapagos/lonesome-george/.

"Lonesome George: Galapagos Tortoise Was the Last of His Kind." National Geographic Education, 2013. Available online at education.nationalgeographic.com/education/media/lonesome-george.

INDEX

Hulse, Carl. "A Giant Tortoise's Death Gives Extinction a Face." *New York Times,* July 3, 2012. Available online at www .nytimes.com/2012/07/03/science/death-of-lonesome-george-the-tortoise-gives-extinction-a-face.html.

Nichols, Henry. *Lonesome George: The Life and Loves of the World's Most Famous Tortoise.* Pan Macmillan, 2007.

UNESCO. "Galápagos Islands." UNESCO World Heritage Centre, 2013. Available online at whc.unesco.org/en/list/1.

White, W. M. "Galapagos Geology: A Brief History of the Galapagos." Geological Department of Cornell, 1997. Available online at www.geo.cornell.edu/geology/GalapagosWWW/Darwin.html.

THE TAMWORTH TWO
"Happy Ever After for Butch and Sundance?" BBC News, 1998. Available online at news.bbc.co.uk/2/hi/uk_news/47671.stm.

"Malmesbury: England's Oldest Borough." BBC History, 2013. Available online at www.bbc.co.uk/history/ancient/anglo_saxons/malmesbury_01.shtml.

"Tamworth Pig." American Livestock Breeds Conservancy, 2013. Available online at albc-usa.org/cpl/tamworth .html.

O'Neill, Sean. "Swimming Boars Save Their Bacon." *Daily Telegraph,* 1998.

O'Neill, Sean. "Pig Knocks the Stuffing Out of Police." *Daily Telegraph,* 1998.

Wilkes, David. "Bye Bye Butch: Tamworth Two Become Tamworth One as Pig Dies 12 Years After Running Off to Avoid the Bacon-Slicer." *Daily Mail Online,* 2012. Available online at www .dailymail.co.uk/news/article-1318984/Tamworth-Two-Tamworth-One-Butch-pig-dies.html.

PHOTO CREDITS

Back cover, Jane Yolen, Heidi Stemple, Adam Stemple, and Jason Stemple photo: Courtesy of the Stemple family; Jui Ishida photo: Cosmo Hebert; 7, Author photo: Courtesy of the Stemple family; 119, Time & Life Pictures/Getty Images; 121, Courtesy smokeybear.com; 149 (top), Arnaldo Magnani/Getty Images; 149 (bottom), Time & Life Pictures/Getty Images; 149 (top), Courtesy the Imperial War Museum; 150 (bottom), Kevin Schafer/Corbis; 150 (top), Time & Life Pictures/Getty Images; 150 (center), Peter Greste/Reuters/Corbis; 151 (bottom), De Agostini/Getty Images; 151 (top), R.E. Foley/New England Aquarium; 151 (bottom), ZUMApress.com/Newscom; 152 (top), Barcroft Media/Getty Images; 152 (center), Archive Photos/Getty Images; 152 (bottom), AP Images/Univ. of Oklahoma; 153 (top), Rex USA; 153 (bottom), Time & Life Pictures/Getty Images; 154 (top), New York Daily News/Getty Images; 154 (center), Time & Life Pictures/Getty Images; 154 (bottom), AFP/Getty Images; 155 (top), New York Daily News/Getty Images; 155 (bottom), Daily Mail/Rex/Alamy

The art for this book is painted in acrylic with digital enhancement. The display font for the book is P22 Dearest, and the body text is set in Sabon LT Std.

PUBLISHED BY THE NATIONAL GEOGRAPHIC SOCIETY
Gary Knell,
President and Chief Executive Officer

John M. Fahey,
Chairman of the Board

Declan Moore,
Executive Vice President; President, Publishing and Travel

Melina Gerosa Bellows,
Publisher and Chief Creative Officer, Books, Kids, and Family

PREPARED BY THE BOOK DIVISION
Hector Sierra,
Senior Vice President and General Manager

Nancy Laties Feresten,
Senior Vice President, Kids Publishing and Media

Eva Absher-Schantz,
Design Director, Kids Publishing and Media

Jay Sumner,
Director of Photography, Kids Publishing

Jennifer Emmett,
Vice President, Editorial Director, Kids Books

R. Gary Colbert,
Production Director

Jennifer A. Thornton,
Director of Managing Editorial

STAFF FOR THIS BOOK
Jennifer Emmett,
Project Editor

David M. Seager,
Art Director

Hillary Leo,
Associate Photo Editor

Ariane Szu-Tu, Paige Towler,
Editorial Assistants

Erica Holsclaw,
Special Projects Assistant

Allie Allen, Sanjida Rashid
Design Production Assistant

Margaret Leist,
Photo Assistant

Carl Mehler,
Director of Maps

Sven M. Dolling,
Map Research and Production

Grace Hill,
Associate Managing Editor

Joan Gossett,
Production Editor

Lewis R. Bassford,
Production Manager

Susan Borke,
Legal and Business Affairs

PRODUCTION SERVICES
Phillip L. Schlosser,
Senior Vice President

Chris Brown,
Vice President, NG Book Manufacturing

George Bounelis,
Senior Production Manager

Nicole Elliott,
Director of Production

Rachel Faulise, Robert L. Barr,
Managers

*F*or David W. Stemple (Daddy, Dad, Papa)
who took us for walks, hikes, road trips, and boat rides; who helped us find turkeys, whales, hawks, owls, pelagic birds.
Who taught us to sit still and listen, or to call back loudly.
Who never stopped wanting to learn—about everything and anything—and to explore, and to share what he had learned with expert and novice, alike.
All the while, he instilled in each one of us, his family, a love of the natural world.
—JANE, HEIDI, ADAM, & JASON

I dedicate this book for all animal lovers and animals we love.
—JUI

The National Geographic Society is one of the world's largest nonprofit scientific and educational organizations. Founded in 1888 to "increase and diffuse geographic knowledge," the Society's mission is to inspire people to care about the planet. It reaches more than 400 million people worldwide each month through its official journal, *National Geographic,* and other magazines; National Geographic Channel; television documentaries; music; radio; films; books; DVDs; maps; exhibitions; live events; school publishing programs; interactive media; and merchandise. National Geographic has funded more than 10,000 scientific research, conservation, and exploration projects and supports an education program promoting geographic literacy.

For more information, please visit nationalgeographic.com, call 1-800-NGS LINE (647-5463), or write to the following address:

National Geographic Society
1145 17th Street N.W.
Washington, D.C. 20036-4688 U.S.A.

Visit us online at nationalgeographic.com/books

For librarians and teachers: ngchildrensbooks.org

More for kids from National Geographic: kids.nationalgeographic.com

For information about special discounts for bulk purchases, please contact National Geographic Books Special Sales: ngspecsales@ngs.org

For rights or permissions inquiries, please contact National Geographic Books Subsidiary Rights: ngbookrights@ngs.org

Library of Congress Cataloging-in-Publication Data
Yolen, Jane.
National Geographic animal stories : heartwarming true tales from the animal kingdom / by Jane Yolen, Heidi E.Y. Stemple, Adam Stemple, and Jason Stemple.
  pages cm
Includes bibliographical references and index.
ISBN 978-1-4263-1725-5 (hardcover : alk. paper) -- ISBN 978-1-4263-1726-2 (reinforced library binding : alk. paper)
1. Animals--Anecdotes. I. National Geographic Society (U.S.) II. Title.
QL791.Y65 2014
591--dc23
                                                    2014015729

Printed in the United States of America

14/WOR/1